PROFESSIONAL ISSUES IN EDUCATION

GORDON KIRK *editors* BOB GLAISTER

ASSESSMENT
A CHANGING PRACTICE

edited by
SALLY BROWN

with contributions from

Harry Black	Eric Drever
Julie Bowen	Lindsay Mitchell
Sally Brown	Mary Simpson

SCOTTISH ACADEMIC PRESS
EDINBURGH
1988

Published by
Scottish Academic Press Ltd
33 Montgomery Street, Edinburgh EH7 5JX

© 1988 Scottish Academic Press Ltd.

First published 1988
SBN 7073 0515 2

British Library Cataloguing in Publication Data

Assessment: a changing practice.
  (Professional issues in education; 2).
  1. Great Britain. Education. Assessment
  I. Brown, Sally, *1935-*   II. Black, Harry
  III. Series
  379.1'54'0941

  ISBN 0-7073-0515-2

Typeset by Pindar (Scotland) Limited, Edinburgh
Printed by Bell and Bain Ltd., Glasgow

PROFESSIONAL ISSUES IN EDUCATION

NUMBER TWO

ASSESSMENT
A CHANGING PRACTICE

PROFESSIONAL ISSUES IN EDUCATION

CONTENTS

EDITORIAL INTRODUCTION

The title of this new series intends to signal its three main features. Firstly, its general area is education. That term, however, means more than schooling, more than a narrowly instrumental view of a process, and extends beyond the limited notion of an institutional base for activities. Secondly, the topics chosen are matters which excite a good deal of interest and concern, mainly, but not exclusively, because they involve change and development. They are matters on which widely differing views are held: in that sense they are issues. Finally, the series will explore ideas and principles which relate directly to educational practice and to the context in which practices are developed and debated. In that sense the issues raised are professional.

The last few years have seen very significant developments in Scottish education. Much change has taken place so quickly that the process of development has been masked. Equally, practitioners are so busy with the implementation of change in their own practice that they are unaware of developments around the country. If the full benefit from change is to be realised, it is necessary to feed both review and analysis of the process and the product back into the system. This series is an attempt to realise that objective.

The topics will be issues which arise in Scotland, are of critical concern in Scotland, but which will be documented and discussed in a way which makes them equally accessible to an audience furth of Scotland. Indeed, each volume is intended to contribute to the wider educational debate and to inform and enliven the critical discussion of changes in educational practice in Britain and elsewhere. The series should not be seen as a collection of research reports, but rather each volume should draw on research findings and other appropriate resources to offer a readable, lively and rigorous analysis of the issues involved.

PREFACE

The introduction of new ideas and practices in assessment has engendered considerable publicity and activity in the United Kingdom over recent years. When major reforms of this kind are attempted they can bring with them considerable confusion and mountains of documents for teachers and student teachers. The intention of this book is to provide a brief collection of papers which draw on the experience of several people who have been involved for some years in assessment innovation. From the tangle of the extensive developments of the last ten years or so, the different contributions attempt to draw out some of the most salient themes and so to present a picture of assessment which is based on rational aims and processes.

Underlying the whole approach of this book is the premise that assessment must be designed to have substantial use for *educational* purposes. It is not simply a tool for selecting people, with administrative efficiency, for the social roles they will occupy in society. In earlier years the latter was the major concern for assessment, and the desire on the part of some to retain this emphasis has been one reason why the innovations have sometimes seemed overpowering and puzzling: they have attempted to introduce the "new" and retain all the "old" with the burden of work falling on those who have to implement the innovations in the schools and colleges. We hope the following eight chapters will be helpful in unravelling some of the confusion and offering a constructive view of assessment for the future.

I would like to express my appreciation to Harry Black, Julie Bowen, Eric Drever, Lindsay Mitchell and Mary

Simpson for so readily agreeing to contribute to this book.
My thanks are also extended to Sandy Lang and May
Young who so efficiently typed the manuscript.

Sally Brown

7th August 1987

CHAPTER 1

ASSESSMENT: A CHANGING PRACTICE

Sally Brown

Scottish Council for Research in Education

A Scenario for Change

Change can be unsettling, sometimes overwhelming, but it can also be motivating and bring about real progress. In the field of assessment, a great deal of talk over the last decade has been about change and substantial attempts have been made to introduce new practices. Different practices usually reflect different ideological commitments, and one of the most salient features of the movement has been the recognition that assessment, as part of education, must be about promoting learning and opportunities, rather than about sorting people into social roles for society.

There are, of course, those who say that there has been no basic change in assessment practices, and indeed there is evidence of resistance from groups with vested interests in holding on to the past. This tendency to try to hang on to the traditional and tested methods at a time when a new philosophy and practice of assessment is being introduced has resulted, in some circumstances, in confusion and impossible demands on practitioners. However, it is important to emphasise that much valuable and ordered progress has been made in this field. Ideas about assessment are discussed and debated among policy-makers, practitioners and researchers more, and more openly, than in the past, and this has led to greater understanding of its role in, and effect on, the education of young people.

Later chapters in this book attempt to present some of that debate, and to look at ways in which practice and thinking are changing. But first we have to look at the way things were, and at the kinds of questions which were being asked about the traditional assessment system.

The Traditional View of Assessment

It is not so long ago that the notion of "assessment" in schools and colleges carried with it, in the United Kingdom at least, a vision of tests or examinations, certificates and grades or lists of marks. All of these were regarded as very important and as providing objective, reliable and precise measures of achievement. The use to which such measures were put was primarily one of the *selection* of young people for such things as further study, training courses, apprenticeships or careers. This system had the great advantage of administrative simplicity: it made comparisons among individuals (norm-referencing), and everyone knew that a grade B performance was better than a grade C and a mark of 49 was less than 51. It appeared to provide an effective means of sorting out those at the "top", the "middle" and the "bottom", and of directing them towards an appropriate niche in society.

The assessment itself usually was carried out in a formal atmosphere and under strictly controlled conditions. Not all of it was undertaken under the auspices of national examination boards, but schools and colleges tended to try to replicate the boards' strict examination conditions: a large hall with an invigilator, no "cheating", examination "papers", a fixed allocation of time for responding in writing to the questions and the whole exercise undertaken at the end of something (a course, a term, a year or a school career). Teachers in "non-academic" areas of the school curriculum without formal examinations tended to assert that they had no assessment. In some subjects, however, it was acknowledged that skills other than those which can be manifest in written answers may be important, and efforts were made to include practical examinations in, for example, home economics, music and science. Where examination boards took such initiatives, teachers were sometimes asked to administer the practical tests, but in strict accordance with instructions prepared by the board.

There were, of course, a wide range of activities going on in which teachers were trying to find out, often in classrooms and by informal means, what pupils had learned or could do. Employers too were making judgements about what apprentices had achieved. All of this we would now include within the concept of assessment, but that has been the case only in recent years.

Over the last two decades the ideas underlying the traditional concept of assessment increasingly have been questioned, and the last ten years have seen some dramatic changes in practice. This book is concerned with providing a picture of some of that assessment reform from a number of perspectives. The emphasis is on assessment of pupils in the later stages of the compulsory period of education, and of the group beyond the age of sixteen who have not traditionally followed the Scottish Certificate of Education "Highers", or the General Certificate of Education "Advanced Level", route into advanced higher education.

Questioning Past Practice

The questioning of past assessment practice has been of several different kinds. Some of it has been concerned with technical matters and has asked: Are grades and marks reliable? Would another marker, or the same marker on another day, make the same judgement about the performance of a young person? Are the assessments valid? Do they assess all they claim to assess? Are they fair? Do they give recognition for achievement or are they more concerned with sorting people out? Perhaps the most searching questions, however, are about the purposes of assessment. Should the focus be on selection, or can it play a more constructive and educational role? If so, is the traditional form of marks and grades appropriate and adequate? And finally, there is debate about who has control of making and reporting the assessments, and of deciding which young people will have access to the benefits which any system of assessment might offer.

There has always been concern about whether tests and examinations are reliable, valid and fair. A substantial body of work of high technical quality has been undertaken, particularly in North America, which has ensured that much is now known about the conditions under which a group of items constitute a reliable test: that is, one which will give the same assessment of the performance of an individual no matter who marks it, and regardless of whether the individual takes the test this week or next. Objective tests with each item having one right answer are most likely to fill the bill; assessment instruments which have heterogeneous items, and subjective marking procedures (e.g. essays), are much less likely to do so. Indeed, measures of reliability on examination essay marking have sometimes produced results which are alarming, especially when it is remembered that the future career of a young person can depend on the outcome of an argument between two examiners about a grade. To avoid this problem, one approach has been to restrict examination questions to objectively marked items. But this may well distort the set of achievements which are assessed; some things which it is intended young people should learn or be able to do are not amenable to objective testing. The capability to create a literary idea, to understand a complex theory or to generate an imaginative artifact, may not be assessable by such means as answering a multiple choice question, or completing a single answer calculation.

A narrowing down of what is assessed to that which can be accurately measured may engineer some improvement in the reliability of a test, but it is likely to endanger its validity. One may ask what use is a grade or mark which is highly reliable but does not reflect the full range of achievements for which the course or set of experiences is aiming? Where such a grade or mark is used for selecting young people, what confidence can there be in its capability to predict that they will be successful in any subsequent course or career?

At a more general level, traditional tests are seen as having substantial limitations in the extent of their sampling of the variety of competences which it is intended young people should acquire. At one level, it is clear that a three hour examination is an inadequate means of assessing, say, the learning from a two year course. There are, furthermore, some kinds of performance which, in principle, cannot be assessed by traditional examinations, particularly where these are restricted to written tests. The validity of marks and grades as measures of performance in any given area, therefore, has been constrained by the form the assessments have taken. In particular, the assessment of practical skills, personal development, attitudes and performance in contexts other than conventional classrooms and laboratories has been neglected.

The matter of the fairness of assessments has been a continuing and agonising concern. Because the main aim of traditional assessments has been to spread out the performance of candidates (so that selection procedures could be carried out more efficiently), great emphasis was placed on choosing test items so as to maximise discrimination between the performance of the high achievers and those of the low achievers. This resulted in the omission of those items which everyone would get right, and so the lowest achievers were denied the opportunity to show what they were able to do. In some parts of the world this has been further exacerbated by the development of "standardised tests". Standardised tests are designed to spread out the performances and make no pretence to match the curriculum to which any given individual has been exposed. They are general tests within a broad area which discriminate well among the whole population of young people. High discrimination, however, is most effectively achieved by reducing the specific content of items; the greatest discrimination is to be found in those tests which closely resemble content-free IQ tests. As soon as a move is made in that direction, the validity of the test as a measure of *educational achievement* must be in doubt. A valid test of such achievement must clearly reflect all the qualities of which it claims to be a measure, and those qualities will be identified with the substance of the curriculum which has been followed.

Many of the characteristics of assessment in the past have resulted from the dominant purpose towards which it has been directed, i.e. selection. In recent years the question has been raised of whether there are not other, and more important, functions for it to fulfil. Since it is part of the educational process should it not have a more constructive role to play in teaching and learning? Should the very considerable efforts which are put into making assessments not be able to produce more, and more useful, information for teachers, students and others? If other functions are to be fulfilled by assessment, then it is unlikely that the traditional form of grades or marks will be adequate. An important limitation of that form is that while it enables comparisons to be made among the performances of individuals (norm-referenced assessment), it provides no information about *what* has been achieved. Any kind of function for assessment which aims to provide information which will help young people to learn, or teachers to teach, will require an evaluative description of what has been achieved (criterion-referenced assessment).

The question of who should carry out the assessment of young people has not been a matter for debate in the past.

Most frequently it has been assumed that the teacher will be the assessor, although examination for certification (probably seen as the most important manifestation of assessment) has generally been the province of professional examiners. There are obvious constraints on the ability of a professional examiner, who under normal conditions would not see the candidate, to carry out a comprehensive assessment of that young person's capabilities in those areas where he or she has had the opportunity to learn. It has been suggested that the teacher will always be in a better position than the examiner to assess, but would that hold when the young people are out of school on, say, work experience or residential courses? The way in which educational aims have changed over the last few years, so that experiences of this kind are now commonplace in the school or college curriculum, clearly has implications for who should be the assessor. Furthermore, the fact that assessments may be carried out by a variety of people, with a range of perspectives, draws attention to the question of whether it is important to have a single measure of achievement for a young person in a given area, or whether it is more rational to accept that different people assess individuals differently, and that such differences should not be concealed within some compromise overall mark or grade.

The notion of young people themselves being involved in self- or peer-assessment has not been a facet of past practice. More recently the question of whether such involvement would be of value in helping to consolidate learning and to increase self-awareness is frequently mooted. For some aspects of personal and social development, which are currently receiving substantial emphasis in curriculum planning, it might seem that the young people are in the best position to make the judgements which assessment of such qualities calls for.

This debate on the possible inadequacy of the range of qualities assessed by traditional measures and the restrictions on who should carry out those assessments, has been accompanied by concern about the proportion of young people leaving formal education without any record of what they have achieved. The established (and academic) certificate courses were not designed for the whole population and, in any case, were unsuited to the educational aims for many young people. Educational "qualifications", however, have become more and more important. If the curriculum is to develop in various ways to prepare everyone more effectively for their future in work and in society generally, then surely, it has been argued, *all* should have the opportunity to work for a certificate which recognises what has been achieved? And if everyone has the chance to earn a certificate, surely such recognition will have a motivating effect on learning and, perhaps, reduce the alienation from education characteristic of many of the low achievers?

The doubts and dissatisfactions with the traditional concept of assessment have resulted in more than academic debate. There have been substantial changes in practice, and the experience gained has led to greater understanding of the potential and the problems associated with assessment. Assessment now commands a much wider conceptualisation than in the past, and tends to be seen as an important and necessary ingredient of effective teaching and learning. This book attempts to exemplify some of the new approaches to, and contexts for, assessment; it incorporates five interrelated themes which are evident in the innovative thinking in this area over the last decade.

Innovative Themes in Assessment Practice

The first theme concentrates on the way in which the concept of "assessment" has progressed from the traditional notion of "testing" for selection purposes. Assessment is now seen as *a much broader concept and fulfilling multiple purposes*. It is considered to be closely integrated with the "curriculum" (a concept which is itself conceived in very much broader terms than in the past) and its purposes include fostering learning, improving teaching, providing valid information about what has been done or achieved, and enabling pupils and others to make sensible and rational choices about courses, careers and other activities. Evaluation of pupils for various selection purposes will continue, but there have been major efforts to ensure that we progress from the simplistic notion that young people can be put in some kind of rank order by grades (frequently based on the results of a single examination). Assessment, therefore, now has several functions including the diagnosis of causes of young people's success or failure, the motivation of them to learn, the provision of valid and meaningful accounts of what has been achieved, and the evaluation of courses and of teaching. We are much more cautious these days about making claims for how effectively assessment in one context can predict the success of young people in other contexts at later dates. The emphasis has shifted away from assessment for summative purposes: that is a report at the end of a course or period of study which purports to predict future performance. Much more stress is laid on assessment for formative purposes: that is the use of the information gathered to improve the current educational process.

This multiple-purpose concept of assessment, which is closely linked to the totality of the curriculum, leads directly to the second theme. This theme is concerned with the considerable *increase in the range of qualities assessed and contexts in which that assessment takes place*. Stringent boundaries put on many assessment systems in the past are breaking down. No longer is it necessary for the qualities assessed to be "academic" and strictly amenable to measurement. Assessment of personal, social and attitudinal characteristics are frequently under consideration, and what counts as "achievement" within even traditional subject areas has expanded considerably. In addition, the contexts in which assessment takes place are much more diverse than in the past. No longer are examination halls the places which one immediately associates with assessment; long-overdue recognition is being given to the fact that most, and the most valuable, assessment is carried out on the site where the learning takes place. Changes in the curriculum have brought about acceptance that the place of learning is no longer always the school or college. The rise of work experience and community activities, for example, have opened up the issue of assessment for school pupils in the context of the workplace.

For the third theme, attention is directed to the rise of *descriptive assessment*. Much of this has manifested itself in the form of concern for criterion-referenced approaches which replace or complement traditional norm-referenced systems. The aim has been to provide descriptions of what has (or has not) been achieved rather than to rely on pupils' marks or grades which have little meaning other than as a comparison with the marks and grades of others. Descriptions of this kind are seen as having the potential to help us understand what, and why, children are or are not learning, and to facilitate improved learning. Such descriptions may also be able to ameliorate the disadvantages of the competitive traditional system and to promote more cooperative attitudes to learning. Perhaps the most persuasive argument, however, has related to the anticipated value of the descriptive information to teachers and young people in making rational decisions about such things as courses to be followed, curricula to be reformed, work to be done, remediation to be carried out, and so on.

The fourth theme is concerned with the *devolution of responsibilities for assessment* to, for example, schools, teachers, work experience employers and young people themselves. Teachers have always carried out most of the assessment to which pupils and students are subjected, but traditionally the assessment which "matters" (i.e. national certification) has been firmly in the hands of external examination boards. The recognition that at all levels internal assessment by educational institutions is of crucial importance is changing all that; but things are going further in some quarters. The concern with the assessment of a wider range of things some of which, like work experience, happen outside the classroom has led to the involvement of others, such as employers, in the assessment process. Furthermore, many of the arguments about the value of assessments to pupils themselves have suggested that the benefits will be greatest if the young people can be persuaded to undertake self-assessment.

The fifth and final theme focusses on assessment for certification. Much of the public debate and changes in government policy in the eighties have supported the view that *certification should be available to a much greater proportion of the population of young people* than has been the case in the past. The nature of certification is also undergoing reform. Thus we have such examples as the new General Certificate of Secondary Education (GCSE) in England and Wales, and the Standard Grade and the National Certificate in Scotland. GCSE is directed at a wider range of the population than either of its predecessors (the General Certificate of Education and the Certificate of Secondary Education), Standard Grade is designed to provide a qualification for the whole of the age cohort, and the modular National Certificate programme offers systematic coverage in an area which previously had a rather confusing mixture of different kinds of provision (not to mention large gaps). The notion of school-based, or local authority-based, certificates is also being extended in the experiments on Records of Achievement which are being pursued, particularly in some parts of England and Wales.

The innovations identified in these five themes are by no means restricted to assessment developments in the United Kingdom. Apart from the fifth theme, which reflects the substantially greater obsession with certification in this country compared with most others, there is a considerable and world-wide literature concerned with similar matters. The exemplifications and elaborations of the themes which are given in the following chapters, however, are all British, and mostly from Scotland. In almost every case parallel or similar developments are going on both sides of the Scotland–England border, despite the separation of the two education systems. All of the authors have been engaged for extended periods of time in educational research or development in Scotland, and each of their various studies has had a primary focus on assessment.

It is the case, of course, that researchers and developers are unlikely to change the world unless politicians provide the opportunities for them to do so. For these authors, many of those opportunities have emerged through the analysis and developments following from a small number of government reports over the last ten years. Whatever the quality of those reports, it cannot be denied that they have stimulated changes in assessment practice. It must be added, however, that much of the fundamental thinking, which the government has to call on before such reports can be prepared, is done by people like those who have contributed the following chapters. While they may not always admit it, politicians and researchers/developers need each other.

Of the reports which have particular significance for this book, two are specifically Scottish: *Assessment for All* (i.e. the "Dunning Report") and *16–18s in Scotland: An Action Plan* (Scottish Education Department, 1977 and 1983). Two of the other three are British and are concerned with education and training on both sides of the border: *A New Training Initiative: An Agenda for Action* and *TVEI Review* (Manpower Services Commission, 1981 and 1984). And the fifth report applies to England and Wales: *Records of Achievement: A Statement of Policy* (Department of Education and Science and the Welsh Office, 1984).

The Rest of the Book

Because each of the next six chapters of this book is concerned with extending discussion of several of the five innovative themes, there is no single dimension which it could be claimed develops as one reads through the six. Some, it might be argued, are concerned more with the *process* of assessment and others with the *products*. But it is a matter of emphasis; any discourse on assessment must address matters of both process and product.

In Chapter 2 Mary Simpson tackles the issue of using assessment for purposes of the diagnosis of pupils' learning rather than for selection. As well as a clear exposition of the responsibilities of educators to support learning in this way, she presents a critique of the cavalier use by writers on assessment of the word "diagnosis", and questions whether that word is appropriately applied to many of the classroom procedures which are labelled as "diagnostic assessment". She argues that such procedures cannot fulfil their intended function unless they are informed about how young people learn and how that learning can go wrong. Her account leads the reader through much of the information available from research in this area in the context of pupils' learning in secondary school science, particularly among the fourteen to sixteen age group. This forms a basis for the suggestions she provides on how pupils' learning difficulties may effectively be diagnosed.

While Chapter 2 demonstrates how important it is to take cognisance of research findings when planning assessment, Lindsay Mitchell in Chapter 3 starts from very practical matters and focuses on new contexts for, and new forms of, assessment. Her experiences of assessment in environments other than the school (and in particular in the workplace) draw attention to the different kinds of demands and constraints that impinge on the assessor and the assessed in those circumstances. She presents her arguments in relation to young people undergoing vocational education and training in the government's Youth Training Scheme. The assessment of "real" behaviour in a "real" context, in contrast with the cloistered environment of school assessment, brings its own challenges not the least of which is the lack of experience among both those whose responsibility it is to design accreditation schemes and those who have to carry out the procedures.

Julie Bowen, in Chapter 4, considers the transfer of responsibility for the assessment procedures to yet a different group: the young people themselves. She looks closely at the arguments for the value of pupils and students being involved in the process, and at the details of the process itself. The second part of the chapter provides an account of self-assessment within a development in the government's *Technical and Vocational Education Initiative*, and demonstrates how the process leads to an assessment product in the form of a profile rather than the traditional single mark or grade.

The matter of profiles and records of achievement (ROA) is continued into Chapter 5 by Sally Brown and Harry Black. They explore the nature and history of these forms of assessment, and discuss the educational benefits which have been claimed for this approach over traditional procedures. This is followed by a summary of evidence available on the implementation of ROAs in schools (through the initiative by the Department of Education and Science) and comment on the range of questions which remain to be resolved if ROAs are, in practice, to fulfil their theoretical potential of providing valid, meaningful and useful descriptions of what has been achieved or experienced.

In Chapter 6, Eric Drever also takes up the matter of how a change can be made so that reports of assessment provide helpful accounts of what has been achieved. His context, however, is the development in the secondary school of Standard Grade in the Scottish Certificate of

Education. He examines the implications of moving to a criterion-referenced system for certification, and analyses the effects of the decision to use Grade Related Criteria as a means of doing this. The escalating complexity of the system following this decision is mapped out, and the consequences of choosing a scheme, which appeared to combine the advantages of both norm-referencing and criterion-referencing at a stroke, are all too clear. Nevertheless, he concludes with some positive hope for the future.

Harry Black too is concerned in Chapter 7 with criterion-referenced certification but in a different context and form. His context is the modular curriculum for the National Certificate in Scotland. This innovation is, for the time being, most apparent in further education colleges rather than schools. He discusses the assessment model which has been introduced and which is based on a series of mastery/non-mastery decisions for each module of the curriculum. His account of the new assessment practices in this sphere of education demonstrates very well how relevant they are to all five of the innovative themes which this book is emphasising.

The final Chapter 8 returns to the five innovative themes. It examines the evidence on each of them which is to be gleaned from the different perspectives of the authors of Chapters 2 to 7. Can it be inferred that assessment is a changing practice? If so, how far has it still to go to achieve the aims of the new philosophies? Or is it really just all show, with the same old testing and grading procedures being dressed up to look new?

REFERENCES

Department of Education and Science and the Welsh Office (1984). *Records of Achievement: A Statement of Policy*, London: HMSO.

Manpower Services Commission (1981). *A New Training Initiative: An Agenca for Action*, Sheffield: HMSO.

Manpower Services Commission (1984). *TVEI Review*, Sheffield: MSC.

CHAPTER 2

THE DIAGNOSTIC ASSESSMENT OF PUPIL LEARNING

Mary Simpson
Northern College of Education, Aberdeen Campus

Introduction

There is perhaps no word which is more abused in the educational literature than the word "diagnostic". Classroom tests and other assessments are claimed to be diagnostic when they do no more than identify those particular tasks on which the pupil fails, or the particular subject areas which the pupil does not understand. But the word "diagnose" is not a synonym for "identify", it means literally "to know between", that is to say, to distinguish or to differentiate. When we complain of stomach pain, we do not expect our physician merely to identify the precise area of our body in which the pain occurs and to prescribe pain killers. We expect him to diagnose our problem: to distinguish between the possible causes, whether appendicitis or over-indulgence, and then to prescribe a treatment which is appropriate not just to the symptom, but to its cause. Similarly, when pupils are found on examination to show the symptoms of "failure to learn", they are entitled to expect more from diagnostic assessment than a description, however precise, of the area in which their failure occurred; they know well enough for themselves what subjects or topics they have difficulty in understanding, and they are entitled to have the underlying causes of this lack of success properly diagnosed and professionally dealt with.

In this chapter, I shall argue that we now have sufficient understanding of the ways in which learning occurs and can go wrong to allow a genuine diagnosis of the reasons for learning failure, a prescription for remediation and an effective policy for prevention.

The Changing Remit for Assessment

For most of their professional lives, teachers have been required to use assessments to answer norm-referenced questions of the kind—"Who is best?", and "Who is worst?" in order to respond to the implicit question "Who can be predicted to do well and who badly in the future?". The value which society attached to examination results led to their veneration as totem objects by pupils, parents and employers, despite the fact that their actual power to predict future performance was slight (save perhaps for those tasks demanding the same learning skills, and to be performed under the same conditions). The situation was clearly unsatisfactory. Pupils classified as "worst" were demotivated and consequently became disaffected with school life. Teachers became unsure of what they were trying to teach or how to improve learning; employers were critical of the unreliability of certificates as indicators of what pupils could be expected to know or do. Things were in a mess simply because we were attempting a particular task, the sorting of pupils, which had no real validity and which subverted us from our responsibility as educators to endow pupils with the framework of knowledge which will support further learning, and with the confidence and wish to pursue it.

In 1977 the members of the Dunning committee identified and recommended a radically different purpose for assessment in the third and fourth years of secondary school:

> "4.2 The essential requirements of the assessment system are firstly that it should be a positive aid to the

improvement of the performance of each individual, and secondly that it should provide guidance on the courses to be followed through school and on the selection of a career." (Scottish Education Department, 1977)

Assessment, they believed, *should not be intended to sort pupils, but to serve them.* It should, therefore, no longer be norm-referenced but criterion-referenced, providing a continuous monitoring of what each pupil "knows and can do". The recommendations of the Dunning committee were accepted by the Government and lay at the heart of the Scottish Certificate of Education Standard Grade development now being implemented in schools. Only some parts of the development, however, can be considered to be educationally useful.

The requirement that teachers should specify, in some detail, the learning outcomes of each course and of each topic area undoubtedly has led to a more careful planning of course content, and the evaluative use to which criterion-referenced assessment was put has resulted in a reappraisal of methods of course presentation. However, almost all the time, energy and inventiveness of the developers was devoted to those details of assessment which are involved in its use as a sorting instrument, little or no attention was paid to the development of assessment for diagnostic purposes and no exemplars of diagnostic assessment procedures were offered in the guidelines subsequently produced for any Standard Grade subject. The development thus substantially retreated from the intentions of the Dunning committee:

"8.2 For example, it is insufficient to devise curricular objectives and to find out whether they have been attained by each pupil; for those who are not successful the reasons for misunderstandings require to be identified and alternative methods adopted." (Scottish Education Department, 1977)

School-based Diagnostic Assessment: What Developed?

It was not the role of the Dunning committee to give teachers detailed guidance on how to develop effective diagnostic assessment procedures or how to manage them within the classroom; that task devolved to Joint Working Parties (JWPs) of experts including some teachers. However, the various Guidelines which the JWPs produced were uninformative on the topic of diagnostic assessment, even when they specified that it should be "obligatory". In the absence of authoritative advice it was predictable that any procedures which were developed in schools would be rooted in already familiar classroom procedures.

The best of school practice in diagnostic assessment (see issue 20 in 1983 of *Programmed Learning and Educational Technology*), involved the identification of intended learning outcomes, the specification of criterial levels of attainment, the identification of core content for each topic area and the writing of extension and remedial materials. Such procedures serve to define the areas in which a pupil may experience learning difficulties, but do not diagnose the cause of those difficulties. They ignore the possibility that the source of difficulty may lie outside the topic area and, far from being an innovation, amount to no more than a formalisation of what good teachers are already doing.

The limited diagnostic usefulness of tests which are referenced to course objectives is revealed by the kinds of remediation to which they point. "Training to get the answers right" consists in reviewing test results with the class and getting the low scorers to repeat the test, often after a brief recapitulation of the subject material by the teacher, in the hope that pupils will rethink their answers. A second form of remediation, the remedial loop, consists in requiring the failing pupil to work through similar though perhaps simplified material, often accompanied by exhortations to "revise at home", "to concentrate more" or to "work harder".

There are undoubtedly some inattentive or work-shy pupils for whom the remedial loop and advice to revise or do extra homework is appropriate, but such advice to the majority of pupils who are failing to understand is an inadequate response to their learning difficulties and merely adds insult to their already injured learning processes. If we are to help pupils to achieve more than they presently do, we need to devise far more effective diagnostic procedures than criterion tests referenced to course objectives, and we must ensure that both assessment procedures and teaching procedures are better informed by an accurate knowledge of how learning takes place and can go wrong.

How Learning Takes Place and can Go Wrong

Much of what takes place in our schools, and is considered important in educational research and in colleges, appears to reflect an underlying belief that it is teaching rather than learning that is the most important activity in the classroom, and that learning is merely an epiphenomenon: the naturally expected outcome if the pupil pays attention to what the teacher says and does, and is diligent in performing the given tasks. This attitude is not surprising since it is only comparatively recently that an understanding of the mechanisms involved in learning has started to emerge, largely as a result of research in cognitive psychology and other cognitive sciences.

The details of these mechanisms need not concern us here, but, broadly speaking, learning can be described as involving two processes: the establishment of information in long-term memory stores, and the constant, on-going matching of incoming information with the contents of the store. The information in the store comprises highly personal representations of experience as discrete "packages" of information about generically related experiences of, for example, objects, actions and feelings; about the relationships between the components within each "package" or schema, and about the relationships between the schemata. Established schemata can be modified but cannot be erased, like a computer tape, except by severe physiological damage. Through the match/mismatch process, sensory inputs to the brain are constantly tested and evaluated for fit with the information encoded in long term memory. Meaningful learning is the result of the interaction of these two processes.

If the new incoming information is wholly congruent with a schema in long term memory, it is incorporated into that schema, and thereby gains all that schema's encoded generalisations and associations; the information is thus understood in terms of what the learner already knows. This learning by accretion is the common method by which we acquire information and attach meaning to it.

If the new information *almost*, but not fully, fits what is encoded in the schema, adjustments take place in the structure of the schema and the new and old information is understood in terms of the content of the modified schema. It is this form of learning which is involved in concept development.

If the degree of incongruence of the new input is so great that it cannot be accommodated by the "fine tuning" described above, a new schema may be generated, incorporating some but not all features of the old and new information. It is this process which is involved in radical concept change. The learner will then have two alternative, competing schemata against which incoming information will be tested for match/mismatch.

If incoming information is so novel, or is structured in such a way that no links can be made with material already encoded in the schemata, it can be acquired only by rote learning. It will be incorporated into memory by dint of repetition, but will have made no significant meaningful links with other established and well understood material. It will be more readily forgotten, and will be unavailable for use as meaningful knowledge in problem solving situations.

This theory of learning does not rely on concepts such as limitations in "ability" to explain learning failure. It suggests, instead, that success in any learning context is primarily dependent on the content and structure of what the pupil already knows.

If what the pupil knows is erroneous, those errors will be incorporated into what is learned, if it has deficiencies, what is learned will have the same deficiencies. If what the pupil knows is badly structured, that is by being erroneously or inadequately related to knowledge in other topic areas, then what the pupil subsequently learns will also be badly structured and will limit further learning.

Learning is similarly dependent on the structure and content of the material to be learned and on the clarity with which it can be perceived by the learner. If the salient features of the content do not articulate with what the pupil already knows, meaningful learning will not occur. If it omits key information, uses potentially misleading analogies or makes simplifications which result in anomalies or contradictions, then what is taught will not be comprehensible to the learner. If its significant features are embedded in activities and peripheral information, pupils may be unable to understand the message because it is obscured by too much "noise".

Finally, if what is taught does not take account of what the pupil has learned outside school, the pupil will misunderstand and the teacher will be unable to understand why the pupil is so stuck.

According to this model, learning is a continuous activity which is the same whether it takes place out of school or in the classroom. It can occur correctly or can result in the learner gaining an idiosyncratic and erroneous understanding of what is taught. When it does go wrong it is much easier to correct early rather than later since the more frequently a faulty schema is used, the more likely it is to be selected as the template for organising and acquiring new information.

How may Pupil Learning Difficulties be Diagnosed?

The questions in any assessment which is genuinely diagnostic differ from those in other forms of assessment in requiring *teachers* rather than pupils to find the answers. If the sources of learning failure are to be identified and adequately responded to, the teacher has to answer four central questions: What has the pupil actually learned, right or wrong, from my teaching? Why did what was learned make more sense to the pupil than what I intended? What was it in the pupil's experience which caused erroneous learning? What was it in what was taught which caused him or her to misunderstand?

What Has the Pupil Learned, Right or Wrong?

During the course of a series of studies of the origins of pupil learning difficulties and pupil misconceptions in biology (Simpson and Arnold, 1984) we encountered two parallel and widespread misconceptions among teachers. The first was that they already knew what were their pupils' difficulties. In fact, we found that their perception of what were the difficult and what were the easy aspects of some of the topics they were teaching was often quite erroneous and their knowledge of what their pupils had actually learned was often deeply flawed. Indeed their common response when confronted with our findings of what their pupils actually thought was the indignant "But I didn't teach them that!", as if pupils were expected to learn only in school, to learn only as intended, and to learn only what they had been taught. The second misconception was that the traditional end-of-topic tests, referenced to course objectives, will tell them what pupils have actually learned. They do not.

As commonly applied, end-of-topic tests tell us how much our pupils remember of what they have been taught, but they do not tell us what they actually know. Diagnostic assessment requires us to use a framework of reference which reflects a realistic appreciation of what actually happens in the course of education: that is although we may present the same information to all the pupils in our class, they will understand it in different ways, creating different and personal knowledge structures according to their different histories of learning and instruction, and to their different (and substantially unknown) out of school experience. If we are to use such tests for diagnostic purposes, our concern must be less with the correctness of a pupil's answers than with the way in which they reveal what the pupil knows, and how she or he thinks. Wrong answers are commonly more informative than right answers.

Some pupil errors in end-of-topic tests will be found to be mere slips such as computational errors, or errors of fact (e.g. that water boils at 100°F), and call for no remediation other than correction.

More commonly, it will be found that some pupils answer erratically, giving correct answers to some questions, but responding incorrectly to others which are substantially similar but are set in a different context. This is a clear indication that the material has been rote learned and that the pupils have gained no meaningful understanding.

Other errors will be found to be widespread within the class. It is common, for example, for pupils to have misunderstood from their lessons in biology, that plants don't respire, or do so only in the dark; in physics, that gravity causes heavy objects to fall faster than light ones; in computing, that computers behave like "reasonable human beings". When the prevalence of these kinds of misconceptions has been recognised, they should be specifically tested for by including appropriate items in the tests.

Even the best designed tests, however, will not reveal the diversity of knowledge which has been constructed by pupils. If we are to explore this, we must listen non-judgementally to what they have to tell us in their own informal language. We will be startled to discover how bizarrely they have learned from what they have been taught. For example, in lessons on photosynthesis, pupils are taught that plants absorb a gas (CO_2) from the air and convert it under the influence of light and chlorophyll into food in the leaves. Many pupils actually learn that the gas is absorbed into the plants through the roots.

Pupils are taught, in chemistry, that all "matter" is made of atoms and molecules, and, in biology, that living things are made of cells. Answers to assessment questions reveal that what many actually learn is that inanimate objects (including heat, light and energy) are made of atoms and molecules, and living things are made of cells, apart from the "non-living" parts (hair, teeth, nails, fins) which are made of atoms and molecules.

Pupils are taught, in mathematics, the correct procedures for multiplication and division. What they often actually learn is that multiplication always makes the number larger, and division smaller. While correctly computing the sum $\frac{1}{3} \times \frac{1}{2} = \frac{1}{6}$, they believe $\frac{1}{6}$ to be the largest fraction of the three; and in dividing 4 by $\frac{1}{2}$ they "know" the answer to be 2.

Misconceptions of this kind are not revealed by the usual kinds of end-of-topic tests which are referenced to the course objectives, and they are almost invariably overlooked by the classroom teacher. They would become more apparent if end-of-topic tests were to be more loosely framed, taking account of the variety of ways in which pupils may form understandings of what they are taught. But ultimately, their detection is dependent on pupils' talk playing a much more significant part in normal classroom activities.

Clearly, undetected and therefore uncorrected misconceptions can act as powerful blocks to the understanding of school knowledge. Kent (1978) gives a particularly vivid account of this blocking effect in his description of "Margaret", a mature and highly motivated student who thought she couldn't do algebra (presumably her former teachers agreed), and whose difficulty was finally traced, during a long discussion, to her understanding that $3x$ meant "thirty something"! Perhaps we should reflect on the probability that for every Margaret who is sufficiently determined to seek help and fortunate enough to find the teacher with time and patience to discover the source of her difficulties, there may be dozens of Jeans and Johns who settle for the diagnosis that they just "can't do" certain subjects.

Why Did What Was Learned Make More Sense to the Pupil Than What Was Intended?

Pupils are not unreasonable, nor are they unreasoning. If they have understood wrongly or, if denied understanding, have colluded by attempting to learn by rote, it is for good reasons. Their behaviour has not been arbitrary and capricious, but predictable. Prior to the course they may have gained undetected misconceptions which made misunderstanding inevitable, or they may have had critical gaps in their knowledge which resulted in a different understanding from what was intended; alternatively, what was taught may have been so poorly structured as to preclude any attachment to what pupils already knew, may have contained anomalies, or been so obscured by non-essential information as to prevent the message being accurately received. The many investigations of pupil learning difficulties, particularly in science and mathematics, have provided abundant evidence of all these causes of learning failure.

But perhaps the biggest source of learning difficulties lies in the failure to define, with any degree of precision, what it is that pupils need to know before starting a new course and to ensure by assessment and by provision of appropriately directed remediation that they have that prerequisite knowledge. *If pupils do not have all the knowledge necessary to understand what they are taught, idiosyncratic learning is inevitable.* Much school policy appears to reflect a belief that, for example, because pupils in a newly assembled class have previously "done" living things, solids, liquids and gases, though perhaps with different teachers, they will have all the information necessary to understand the Scottish Certificate of Education "O" grade topic of photosynthesis. In fact, a study of learning difficulties in this topic area (Simpson and Arnold, 1982) reveals that more than one third of certificate biology pupils used the words and images characteristic of primary pupils to describe a gas, most were no better than primary pupils in their classification of living and non-living things, half did not know the distinguishing characteristics of living things (e.g. reproduction, respiration, excretion) and carbon and carbohydrates were misclassified as gases by one third. It is not surprising that such pupils have difficulty in gaining the intended knowledge about the relationships between plants, respiration, carbohydrates, photosynthesis and the plant's need for food.

As already suggested, learning may be impeded by unremedied misconceptions. In terms of the learning theory, *if what the pupil already knows within a topic area is incorrect, those errors will be incorporated into what is subsequently learned* in that area. "O" grade pupils who have learned that the molecules of a dissolved solid fit into the spaces between the water molecules come to "know", undetected by their teachers, that:

substances are insoluble because their molecules are too big to fit into the spaces (57 per cent of certificate pupils) the molecules of a dissolved solid are not evenly spread throughout the solution (83 per cent)

the molecules of water and of glucose exist in a variety of sizes (54 per cent and 52 per cent respectively)

there is no change in volume when sucrose is dissolved in water (42 per cent).

Such pupils predictably find the teachers' account of osmosis (which relies on correct knowledge of concentration, solutions and molecular sizes) extremely confusing and ambiguous.

What Was It in the Pupils' Experience Which Caused Erroneous Learning?

Learning is a constant, not an occasional activity, it does not take place only at school, or even largely in the classroom. Pupils have continuous life experiences during which they accumulate information about the world they live in and formulate personal explanations for the phenomena they have encountered. These explanations, termed "alternative frameworks", "naive knowledge", or "buggy algorithms", cause particular problems for both the learner and the teacher. They are used by the pupil to interpret what is subsequently taught, and they are commonly unknown to the teacher, who cannot understand why the pupil is finding difficulty or appears to be learning so capriciously.

One of the most disconcerting features of alternative frameworks is their extreme persistence. They are commonly resorted to even by experienced scientists when answering under pressure, and seem to be highly resistant to change. This can be interpreted in the following way. The learner, as a result of life experiences, has developed a schema for a particular topic (which often continues to receive reinforcement from out of school sources) and as a result of school learning experience develops a second schema for the same topic. Since schemata cannot be erased, the learner is able to interpret further experiences (or respond to problems) *either* in the light of the original "naive" schema, *or* of the "school" schema. The most effective strategy open to the teacher is to try to decrease the likelihood of the pupil using the "naive" schema by ensuring that the school-based knowledge is made more plausible, comprehensible and useful.

What Was It in What Was Taught Which Made Pupils Fail to Learn What Was Intended?

Investigators of learning difficulties have consistently reported, not by way of criticisms of teachers but of the curriculum, that the content of what is taught in secondary schools is often poorly structured and not infrequently ambiguous or obscure. For good learning, not only must pupils be prepared to receive the teacher's message, but the message itself must be clear, coherent and free from ambiguity. It is, therefore, of critical importance for improvement in learning that teachers should question the comprehensibility and coherence to the novice of what they teach.

Progress in learning is dependent on, and indeed may comprise, the steady development and elaboration of basic concepts by the learner. Considerable lip-service is paid to this process in the terminology used by curriculum developers in the statement of course objectives but its importance is normally indiscernible in the actual content of courses. A scrutiny of teaching material and texts, including those for the recently introduced Standard Grade course shows that, far from providing any instruction in concepts, they present a wide range of information and assume that pupils will derive the concepts for themselves. What is critically absent is any identification of the concepts to be derived and any formal consideration of examples and non-examples the concepts, their critical and non-critical attributes, and their super- and subordinate characteristics. It is interesting, for example that the few "O" grade biology pupils, who by their answers to test questions showed that they had gained mastery in the classification of "living things", "things made of atoms and molecules" and "things made of cells", when interviewed and asked whether they had gained their knowledge in school, gave replies such as "I think it was just general knowledge, watching TV". The implied indictment of the curriculum is that if we wish to remedy or prevent pupils' learning difficulties in biology we should advise them to spend more time watching TV!

When we know something well, we infer information which is missing, overlook contradictions and reject distractions without being aware of doing it. It is indeed the very knowledgeability of specialist teachers which makes it difficult for them to recognise the ambiguities and sources of confusion in what they teach. However, whenever subjects in secondary school have been subjected to the scrutiny of researchers, they have invariably been found to be rich in anomalies, contradictions, gaps and other learning traps for the innocent learner.

If we are to diagnose the ways in which the content of what is taught causes pupils to learn badly, we must try to set aside our expertise and put ourselves into the position of learners. We might even ask the opinions of "naive" colleagues from other disciplines.

Implications of Diagnostic Testing for the Future

The expectancies of pupil learning outcomes by teachers and curriculum planners are essentially norm-referenced, because their experiences have been essentially norm-referenced. A few pupils learn well, a few badly, and most lie somewhere in the middle. Until comparatively recently, these expectancies were considered reasonable and explicable in terms of differences in "intelligence", "levels of formal reasoning" and motivation or application.

The introduction of genuinely diagnostic forms of assessment is likely to change such expectancies. We will become increasingly aware that although under some future ideal forms of instruction, intrinsic differences may indeed set some limits on learning achievements, many of the difficulties which pupils presently encounter in trying to understand specialist subjects are the result, not of deficiencies in the pupils, but of certain characteristics of the content of previous and present courses. We will find ourselves in agreement with Anania (1983) that

> "Individuals possess far greater potential than the majority of them are able to realise because of decisions which have been made about what shall constitute standard school practice."

Obviously we will want to improve the attainments of our present pupils, and indeed we will be in a position to provide better remediation than formerly because it will be targeted to the sources rather than the symptoms of the learning difficulty. But beyond that, we will want to prevent rather than cure the problems. Significantly, it is the response of the specialist subject teacher which offers the best hope for educational change. Such teachers have been criticised in the past for being more interested in teaching their specialist subject, than in teaching children. But, in my experience, when they see evidence from diagnostic assessment that learning difficulties can be traced to the teaching content of their speciality, they become responsive to the need for change. However, responsibility for changes in what constitutes standard school practice in secondary subjects does not lie with the class teacher, but with curriculum planners.

In this chapter I have suggested that in any assessment which has a genuine diagnostic purpose, some questions are addressed to pupils, and some to class teachers. The following, more fundamental questions should be directed to the curriculum developers.

What knowledge, concepts and skills must pupils have if they are to engage successfully with the learning experiences offered in the new course?

What relevant knowledge, concepts and skills have actually been provided by previous courses?

What misconceptions can be predicted to arise during the presentation of this material? How can the development of these misconceptions be avoided?

What "alternative frameworks" are pupils likely to have in these topic areas?

Is the evidence clear that the selected learning experiences are the appropriate vehicles by which pupils can attain the intended learning outcomes?

In the development of our current secondary school courses, there is little evidence that any of these questions were seriously addressed. If we continue to excuse the planners, developers and implementers from the application of diagnostic assessment to their own activities, we will, alas, continue to fail the pupils.

REFERENCES

Anania, J. (1983). "The influence of instructional conditions on student learning and achievement", *Evaluation in Education, An International Review Series*, 7 (i), 1–81.

Kent, D. (1978). "Some processes through which mathematics is lost", *Educational Research*, 21 (i), 27–35.

Scottish Education Department (1977). *Assessment for All (The Dunning Report)*, Edinburgh: HMSO.

Simpson, M. and Arnold, B. (1982). "Availability of prerequisite concepts for learning biology at certificate level", *Journal of Biological Education*, 16 (1), 65–72.

Simpson, M. and Arnold, B. (1984). *Diagnosis in Action*, Occasional Paper No. 1, Aberdeen: Aberdeen College of Education.

CHAPTER 3

NEW CONTEXTS FOR, AND NEW FORMS OF, ASSESSMENT: ASSESSMENT IN THE WORK PLACE

Lindsay Mitchell

Competency Testing Project (Scotvec)

Assessment of the "Real" Thing

Assessment in the work place is assessment of "real" behaviour in a "real" context. It seeks to provide evidence of what people actually can do in a natural setting by assessing performance in ongoing activity. As the assessment is incorporated into the work process less sampling is necessary and it is theoretically possible to assess a greater range of competence over a greater number of occasions. The competence displayed is also that actually required in work rather than that hypothetically thought necessary or tested because of tradition. It thus should have the advantage of being adaptable and responsive to evolving requirements. Issues in the introduction of a criterion-referenced work place assessment system are essentially the same as those in other environments such as classrooms. However, many of them are heightened because of the diversity of the sites, the differing primary functions of the key personnel and the range of competence to be assessed.

This chapter explores the reasons for increasing moves to assess in the work place, what it is that will be assessed, with whom the responsibility for assessment is to lie and the particular problems of formal accreditation. Its focus is the

Youth Training Scheme (YTS) although this is only one of the key developments in the field, which also includes the accreditation of competence wherever it is gained and the assessment of prior learning.

A New Context for Assessment

In the past vocational education and training have tended to be divorced from one another with education providing and assessing the knowledge element, and training the skills. Knowledge has been assessed in written tests, which have tended to test recall of facts, while skills have been assessed as discrete elements rather than constituent parts of the work role. Much of the practical skills testing has been undertaken by the statutory Industry Training Boards (ITBs), who may be considered to be examining/validating bodies in their own right. The vast majority of this testing has taken place in simulated test environments with one-off assessments of skill (e.g. Road Transport Industry Training Board, 1983; and Construction Industry Training Board, 1986). This has gradually replaced, or been combined with, the more traditional apprentice model where assumptions of all-round competence were based on a period of time-serving within industry.

Assessment of work-based learning, therefore, is not new. What is different is the move to formalise the ongoing assessments made by employers, supervisors and peers in the work place itself. That is, to broaden the scope of the competence assessed to include the application of skills and knowledge in purposeful activity, to ground this competence on the standards expected in employment and to contextualise the assessment so that it truly reflects the conditions, pressures and demands needed to perform in the work role. The next section explores the changes made in vocational education and training and the resultant effects on the assessment system.

The Background

The increasing economic ills of the country from the early 1970s onwards, unleashed a torrent of questioning about training for employment and updating. In 1981 the government published the *New Training Initiative* (NTI), which aimed to secure the modernisation of occupational training through three major objectives:

"1. We must develop skill training, including apprenticeship, in such a way as to enable people entering at different ages and with different educational attainments to acquire agreed standards of skill appropriate to the jobs available and to provide them with a basis for progression through further learning.
2. We must move towards a position where all young people under the age of 18 have the opportunity either of continuing in full-time education or entering a period of planned work experience combined with work-related training and education.
3. We must open up widespread opportunities for adults, whether employed, unemployed or returning to work, to acquire, increase or update their skills and knowledge during the course of their working lives." (Manpower Services Commission, 1981)

These objectives and the principles upon which they are based have had profound effects on the vocational education and training system in Britain as a whole, and in Scotland in particular (see Chapter 7 for a discussion of the National Certificate within the Action Plan). Inherent to NTI is the view that training should be available to all. It should be responsive to individual needs, relevant, cost-effective and easily accessible. In particular assessment should be of competence based on agreed standards, rather than the attendance of fixed courses or time serving. The belief is that in this way "a more versatile, readily adaptable, highly motivated and productive work force" would result (Manpower Services Commission, 1984).

One of the major, and perhaps the most prominent, outcome of NTI (Objective 2) has been the development of the Youth Training Scheme (YTS) which heralded a shift in the philosophy of vocational training and education from learning by instruction to learning through experience. The scheme provides up to two years of work related training on a training allowance for all those under the age of 18 who wish to enter. In March 1985, the government announced that the YTS was to become a permanent training programme and to be extended from one to two years (from 1 April 1986), with an emphasis on providing opportunities for all trainees to seek vocational qualifications (Manpower Services Commission, 1985).

While work-based, YTS consists of two interrelating locational elements: the work place and off-the-job. The extended programme increased the proportion of time spent in the work place (from 37 out of 50 weeks to 80 out of 100, i.e. up to 80 per cent from 75 per cent) and the emphasis on qualifications. The Manpower Services Commission (MSC) has thus become under increasing pressure to find valid methods of assessing work place learning and for the full ability range of the population. This, and other MSC initiatives based on NTI philosophy, have had wide implications for the structure of vocational qualifications.

Vocational Qualifications

The White Paper *Working Together—Education and Training* spells out most clearly to date the reforms the government hopes to see in the structure of vocational qualifications (Department of Employment and Department of Education and Science, 1986). It also established a National Council for Vocational Qualifications (NCVQ) which while not involving Scotland in the short term, due largely to Scotland's 16+ National Certificate (NC) reforms, has implications for consultation and co-operation and, in the long term, movement towards common aims. It is stated that "vocational qualifications need to relate more directly and clearly to competence required (and acquired) in work" and that the vocational qualification system "must test and record not just knowledge and understanding but also skills and competence in applying such knowledge. And it must do so in a way which encourages individuals to build on qualifications and to fulfil their potential and stimulates employers to give full recognition for qualifications earned, and therefore standards achieved." YTS should "give every young person taking part the opportunity to obtain a vocational qualification relating to competence in the work place or to obtain a credit towards such a qualification". In addition, a personal record of achievement for each trainee will contribute to a broader assessment of progress.

The new vocational qualifications are to be criterion-referenced to standards required by employment. The National Certificate (16+ Action Plan) while criterion-referenced was drawn from existing types of non-advanced further education qualifications (Scottish Education Department, 1983). Whilst involving extensive discussion with industrial representatives, standards do not necessarily equate absolutely with the range or level of competence objectives required across and throughout industry. MSC has funded, and will continue to fund, work on the identification of standards, using a variety of methods, in order to improve the relationship between, on the one hand, the competence required and training available and on the other hand, the relevance of qualifications to industrial needs (e.g. Hotel and Catering Industry Training Board, 1985; and Clothing and Allied Products Industry Training Board, 1986). This will seek to ensure that not only are standards applicable to industry but that the full range of competences are covered, i.e.

not only those that have traditionally been certificated by education.

As qualifications are to reflect the competence required in industry to the standards of the work place, and with YTS founded on a work-based philosophy of learning, the obvious location for development was the work place itself. What is it, however, that is to be assessed?

Assessment in YTS

YTS is founded on a design framework which is broader than specific job training. Similarly assessment within YTS is more than accreditable qualifications. Much of it is diagnostic and formative with the trainee actively encouraged to self-assess and become aware of his or her own development, competence and needs (see Manpower Services Commission, 1984 and 1986).

This chapter, however, focuses on summative assessment for accreditation and specifically on those qualifications based on work place learning. This is not to deny the importance of either learning and assessment in other contexts (such as off-the-job) or other forms of assessment, but is because of lack of space.

YTS schemes must be founded on the YTS design framework to deliver the four YTS outcomes of:

1. competence in a range of occupational skills;
2. competence in a range of transferable core skills;
3. ability to transfer skills and knowledge to new situations;
4. personal effectiveness.

MSC expresses the belief that together these form a rounded concept of occupational competence (Manpower Services Commission, 1984). This is more encompassing than many traditional industrial views, which tend to focus on specific knowledge and skills to perform in traditional jobs.

Occupational competence has been explained more fully as:

"the ability to perform activities in the jobs within an occupation, to the standards expected in employment. The concept also embodies the ability to transfer skills and knowledge to new situations within the occupational area and beyond to related occupations. Such flexibility often involves a higher level of mastery of skills and understanding than is common among even experienced employees. Competence also includes many aspects of personal effectiveness in that it requires the application of skills and knowledge in organisational contexts, with workmates, supervisors, customers, while coping with real life pressures. Wherever possible, demonstrations of competence will be required under operational conditions to meet the standards required in the new forms of qualifications" (Standards and Assessment Support Unit, 1986a).

A more "handleable" concept of job competence, which could be used as an evaluation tool for vocational qualifications and includes elements of personal effectiveness, is that of Mansfield and Mathews (1985). They state that job competence has three interrelated components of:

tasks (skills used in a routine way);

task management (where there are a number of tasks to do or where tasks require additional activities, i.e. management within and across tasks);

role/job environment (skills of working with people and responding to high criticality factors).

This concept serves to bring together the knowledge and skills required in a job and looks at how these may be demonstrated in practice. "The implication for vocational education and training . . . is that . . . it must include development of skill in all aspects of a job. . . . Traditional concentration on skills needed in individual tasks needs to be balanced by the development of skills of implementing those tasks within a working role" (Mansfield and Mathews, 1985). YTS is broader than this in that it speaks of a range of jobs, i.e. it seeks a broad foundation base so that trainees can transfer competence from one job to another within related occupations.

The technical feasibility of assessing personal effectiveness or ability to transfer is still to be faced. Most of the current development work is concentrating on the practicalities of assessing job competence in the full gamut of industries and with problems such as mobile work places (e.g. fishing boats), seasonal competences (e.g. fertiliser spreading) and industries which are loath to recognise the attributes of those they employ below craft or qualified status. Like the 16+ Action Plan, the work is developing on a modularised basis as this is seen to be the logical means of rationalising provision and of providing flexibility for updating (both modules and individuals). Discussions on whether each module should contain assessment of the four YTS outcomes have not been resolved, a decision to include all four could lead, in the short term, to considerable exclusion since it is envisaged that modules of accreditation will be also suitable for adult workers.

For assessment in the work place to be a reality, units of accreditation will have to reflect a natural grouping of activities for the majority of establishments to which it is relevant, i.e. "be marketable clusters of competence". If individual modules only relate to a few actual work situations they will be unrealistic. The current NC introductory module on Cookery Processes requires basic competence in eleven processes, yet many work places use a maximum of five which are not necessarily the same. This would mean that although trainees were competent in these, at present they could receive no credit. Similarly in Cash Handling many retail outlets cannot cover all methods of payment. Not all work places will possess electronic tills and many do not accept cheques, credit cards or travellers' cheques (Mitchell, 1986).

A major issue for work-based (employment led) learning and accreditation is the tension between the generality or specificity of modules. For example, a particular employer may be interested in the ability to use a specific photocopier. It would be unmanageable for a national accreditation system to provide this service, would lead to a short "shelf-life" for many modules and would inhibit transfer. What is being emphasised in current discussions is the distinction between industry specific competence and company specific competence; the latter is not the realm of a national accreditation system and tends artificially to narrow the education and training debate. Individual companies will of course be able to assess additional competence but this, as in the past, will not be nationally accredited.

Similarly there is tension between the occupational competence currently demanded by employers and the broader concept envisaged by the government. As the Standards and Assessment Support Unit quote made clear this ". . . often involves a higher level of mastery of skills and understanding than is common among even experienced employees", i.e. the underlying aim is to create a more adaptable, versatile work force. Concentration on accreditation of the here-and-now competence demanded in the work place could militate against the very aim that the government seeks. Criteria of performance should be comparable to standards sought in industry as should the competence accredited. It should not, however, be so industrially specific as to inhibit adaptability or transferability, or too narrowly focused as to meet only today's needs rather than tomorrow's. That is it should encourage a system which is constantly open to change and which would provide for the integration of new, developing areas. Also it should not undermine a training system which is based on the principles of adaptability and transferability.

Work Place Supervisor as Assessor

Within YTS, MSC is already utilising the model of assessment by frontline supervisors in the record of achievement. The recent work on the development of accreditation in the work place seeks to build on this and formalise it. It is only one of a number of options which are open (e.g. competency testing is another model) but it makes sense in that supervisors often have charge of YTS trainees and others in the work process and make ongoing informal assessments of competence. Whilst the discussion here focuses on this model it recognises that it would be more desirable to involve other assessors in the process such as the trainees themselves, their peers or cross checking by other supervisors.

Formalised assessment will mean a new role for supervisors and have implications for the design, packaging and type of assessment that can be used. A retail YTS supervisor looking at an existing NC module stated "It's not for the likes of me. I left school at 15 and was never any good at that sort of thing." She, however, was successfully running her own business (Mitchell, 1986). Presentation, layout and language must enhance and encourage the understanding of the users and yet also ensure acceptable levels of validity and reliability. A supervisor-led system, much as any other internally assessed and criterion-referenced system, would necessitate investment in staff development and training. One could anticipate, however, that such an investment would not only benefit the assessment process but likewise the delivery of the training scheme as well. This would not be the case, for example, with external assessors in competency testing situations.

There are some problems with the model proposed because it is based on the assumption of a hierarchical organisation with individuals working one to another. Increasing evidence points to the fact that this may not be as widespread as supposed. YTS trainees may be placed with "supervisors" who are little more than office juniors themselves. On fishing boats, shares and tasks are on a consortium basis with members working as a team (Standards and Assessment Support Unit, 1986b). Similarly, in "caring" contexts much of the work is team based, with outcomes being team rather than individually focused. Such examples of industrial practices raise questions not only of who will carry out the assessment, but the methods by which it can be done.

Conclusions

The operation of a sufficiently reliable and valid criterion-referenced assessment system is not a simple process even in situations where many of the variables are controlled and which contain staff who are trained in the area. To establish such a system across a wide range of locations, which differ markedly and for whose staff the roles of assessment and training are secondary, is a much more complex task. Crediting competence in the work place raises a wide range of issues. Some of these, such as the timing of assessment and moderation, may be peculiar to it. Others, such as assessor self-image and training, level of record keeping required and specification of standards, are common to all criterion-referenced assessment. Extending the system merely heightens and focuses the ever present problems. If the MSC are to meet their aim of modernising occupational training and thus create "a more versatile, readily adaptable, highly motivated and productive work-force" a system of assessing competence, however gained, must be found.

Habitually we connect learning with direct teaching, and thus a programme of instruction. This gives a base on which to nail our assessment. We all know, however, that much of our "important" learning has been developed outside this formal input. For many who have experienced failure in the traditional educational system, work place assessment could provide an acknowledgement of their actual competence in a wider setting. Industry is demonstrating its interest by involvement in research and development work. In one feasibility study, work place assessment was seen by managing agency staff, work place supervisors and trainees as a means of reflecting what trainees could actually do and of contributing to the development of the training programmes (Mitchell, 1986). Formal accreditation of all aspects of a training scheme with interrelating elements forces consideration of each of the parts, of their interrelationships and of the roles of the players within. It thus has the potential to foster learning and increase the learning opportunities. The assessment tail wagging the curriculum dog?

Acknowledgement

I would like to thank Gilbert Jessup, MSC/NCVQ, for helpful discussions in drafting this paper.

REFERENCES

Clothing and Allied Products Industry Training Board (1986). *Standards Project—Progress Report 1985/86 and Outline Proposals 1986/87*, Leeds: CAPITB.

Construction Industry Training Board (1986). *Skills Testing in the Construction Industry*, King's Lynn: CITB.

Department of Employment and Department of Education and Science (1986). *Working Together—Education and Training*, Command 9823, London: HMSO.

Hotel and Catering Industry Training Board (1985). *Caterbase Newsletter*, Wembley, Middlesex: HCITB.

Manpower Services Commission (1981). *A New Training Initiative: An Agenda for Action*, London: HMSO.

Manpower Services Commission (1984). *Guide to the Revised Scheme Design and Content*, Sheffield: MSC.

Manpower Services Commission (1985). *Education and Training for Young People*, London: HMSO.

CHAPTER 4

STUDENT SELF-ASSESSMENT

Julie Bowen
TVEI Unit—Scotland

"Knowing me, knowing you, it's the best I can do." ABBA

The change in the use of assessment away from narrowly selective and predictive intentions towards purposes such as encouraging and informing the learning process has brought the potential of self- and peer-assessment very much into focus in our secondary school sector.

For more than twenty years, practice in the field of vocational guidance and preparation, emphasising personal development, has been giving prominence to self-evaluation as a valuable assessment technique. The present emphasis on student-centred learning, the pilot projects on Records of Achievement in England and Wales, and the advent of the Technical and Vocational Education Initiative (TVEI) are all exhorting the "progressive" educationist to regard Profiling as the "flavour of the 80s". Some of the possibilities and problems concerning Records of Achievement are explored in Chapter 5. When the issues of "how?" and "from whom?" to gather data to complete profile records are addressed it seems impossible to avoid the question of the involvement of the "subjects" of the profiling process in their own assessment.

The first part of this chapter considers three key aspects of the use of self-assessment: the reasons *why* the student could or should be an assessor; *when* in the process it is useful for the student to record self-assessments; and *how* student self- and peer-assessment can contribute effectively to a learning record. The second half of the chapter describes an attempt to set up a profiling system, using student self-assessment in both the formative process and the summative document, within the Fife TVEI project. The final short section comments briefly on the extent to which a student self-assessment does, in practice, provide the student with some control over what is learned and assessed.

Terminology

Before looking at these issues, it is perhaps useful to offer definitions for some of the terms which will be used throughout this chapter.

"Profiling"—is an assessment *process* which involves recording and reviewing of student progress. Profiling records may include information which is objectively measured as well as descriptive information. Recording may be done by the student, or a tutor, or both.

"Profile"—is a summary assessment *document* which provides a picture of a student at a particular point in time. It may be completed by the student, tutor or a combination of tutor and student, and it may contain information validated by others, e.g. an examination board or an employer.

"Formative Assessment"—provides assessment feedback on the learning process as it progresses, allowing students to modify their targets or their approaches to learning. Formative assessment is the basis for the profiling *process*.

"Summative Assessment"—can offer, at any particular stage in a learning process, information on the total knowledge, skills and experience of a student, at that time. A summative assessment may be carried out at a time of change of status (e.g. a school leaver profile) when it is usually described as terminal, or it may be at the end of a term, or year, in which case the summative data can also have some formative use in the following term or year.

"Normative Assessment"—occurs when assessment measures and comments are made or recorded with reference only to the performance of others (e.g. class ordering in tests, "O" Grades in the Scottish Certificate of Education).

"Ipsative Assessment"—is undertaken when the assessment is of progress made by an individual with reference to that particular individual's starting point, regardless of the performance of others.

All of the above terms may be used to describe assessment which is "done to" students (carried out by others) or self-assessment (which is "done by" students).

Why Should Students Self-Assess?

There are sevaral positive arguments which may be advanced about the value of student participation in assessment.

In the first place, such participation may be seen as a support for learning. If the student-centred learning process advocates that students take responsibility for their own learning, then they should also take at least some responsibility for the assessment of that learning. Furthermore, playing an active part in the assessment process encourages students to reflect on their experience and is likely to ensure better consolidation of learning. Their involvement may well motivate and encourage them to be more selective about future learning.

Secondly, there are arguments which suggest that the student is in the best position to make the assessments. If the learning taking place in an increasing number of situations outside the classroom is to be assessed, then the only person who is active in all the situations and can provide a coherent view of all the experiences is the student. This view is supported by approaches which emphasise the value of assessment as descriptive of the "whole" person. Who is more aware and, therefore, in a better position to assess their personal skills, qualities and attitudes than the students themselves?

Thirdly, there is the claim that joint and negotiated approaches to assessment improve the nature and quality of the communication between student and teacher.

Finally, and perhaps most significantly, it may be argued that once people leave the education system they will find that real life situations more often call upon them to assess themselves than provide them with an accompanying assessor.

This list of arguments is not necessarily comprehensive. Others, notably Hitchcock (1986) in her review of the main types of profile which have been devised, have outlined a number of advantages of student recording and student self-assessment. It is worth noting that Hitchcock's definition of "Profile" differs somewhat from the one used in this chapter; she would not accept as a true "Profile" a document which had been completed entirely by a student. Her answer to the "Why?" question seems to be that there are many benefits of student self-assessment provided that it is confined mainly to the formative profiling process with only limited use in the summative profile.

A common criticism of student self-assessment is directed at its lack of objectivity. It is claimed that assessments made by students themselves cannot be considered accurate and are therefore unreliable. This objection is raised particularly with respect to the recording of student self-assessment data on summative profiles. How can such profiles achieve credibility with receivers like employers and higher education agencies? The evidence for these objections is not conclusive. Burke (1969) certainly found that students tended not to assign their own grades accurately, in the view of their teacher; and Cowan (1975) found that university students were unable to determine their best and worst answers to examination questions. However, both these studies were based on situations where the assessment involved was essentially normative. When students are competing with each other, and marks are important, it is not surprising that they tend to over-estimate. In such normative situations, Burke found that peer group assessment or a combination of self- and peer-assessment is likely to prove more reliable than self-assessment alone. At the other extreme, however, when assessment is ipsative (judging individual progress against a particular starting point) then self-assessment can often be the most valid strategy to use.

While it may be accepted that self-assessment has the potential to offer a more valid measure, it is often assumed that external assessment is better because it is more objective and reliable. There is, however, no such thing as total objectivity; all assessments have a subjective, and often normative, element. Even driving test examiners, with their so-called "objective criteria" are influenced by the number of people they have already passed that week and the manner of the testee. No matter how desirable the goal of objectivity is, in most real world situations we have to rely on self-assessment, however subjective. Furthermore, those who have been trained in self-assessment techniques are likely to get better at making self-assessments which are reliable. It seems likely, therefore, that the benefits to be gained from students' self-assessment can outweigh the potential problems involved, provided attention is given to the choice of *what* is being assessed and to the appropriate preparation of students before they are asked to carry out such assessment.

When Should Students Record Self-Assessments?

Once the value of student self-assessment is accepted in principle, it is important to endeavour to gain the best possible results from self-assessment recording. It has been suggested by Hitchcock (1986) that student "self-recording" is "uncompromisingly formative" and has "no summative element". By self-recording she seems to mean the essentially ipsative recording of the type initiated by Stansbury in his Record of Personal Achievement (RPA) (1974) and, in particular, his Record of Personal Experience (RPE) (1984). Hitchcock defines "self-assessment" as involving "a more critical analysis of strengths and weaknesses". This type of assessment, in her view, may have summative value, but is unlikely to be considered sufficient on its own for a summative report. Others have noted the potential tension between the formative and summative elements of the process as far as self-assessment is concerned. Rowntree (1987) states:

> "It is when we step into the firmly summative and credentialising that the student's contribution to assessment becomes problematical."

Some have taken the view that a summative document should not include any student self-assessment at all, as was the case in the original Scottish Council for Research in Education Profile (1977). The rationalisation of such an extreme view is usually in the form of an argument about the audience for a summative profile. Many summative documents have a prime audience of employers and other agencies: people who, it is claimed, want objective information. Other summative records, however, are intended primarily for the use of students themselves, and it is often difficult to reconcile the needs of two very different audiences in the production of one document. As a result, the "external" audience often wins and the student contribution to a final school-leaver profile is frequently minimal.

It is perhaps useful at this point to underline a potential difference in purposes for a summative profile. It may seek to be

a *record* which offers evidence on which judgement may be passed by the audience;

or

a *report* in which judgements have been made and are offered as evidence.

If the purpose of a summative document is to act as a record, then student self-assessment may fit more comfortably into the profile format than if the intention is to provide a more categorical report. In other words, the intended function of the profile document will determine to a great extent the usefulness of student self-assessment data in that document.

The pilot projects involving the development and use of Records of Achievement (ROA) in England and Wales place emphasis on the use of student self-assessment during the formative data gathering period and most summative or terminal documents have a section which can be completed by the student. Rowntree (1987) describes the value of the student's contribution at the summative stage thus:

"Self-assessment and peer assessments can take a proper place alongside teacher assessments and be interpreted sensibly only in a summative assessment whose outcome is not a grade or label but a "profile" of the student to which all who are to speak about him can contribute what they know—and in which conflicting assessments are highlighted rather than ironed out."

It could be said, therefore, that the answer to the "when?" question is that self-assessment has a major formative value but only limited summative or terminal value. This is generally true of the ROA pilots, perhaps because the main audience for the terminal profile is employers or higher education agencies. For students, however, summative documents completed and "owned" by themselves may be highly valued. Certainly the process of completing a summative document may prove very helpful in raising self-awareness and consolidating learning. The self-portrait produced by a profile based mainly on self-assessment can be revealing and could also prove useful to a prospective employer or other agency, if time was taken to understand the procedure.

Referring again to real world experiences, summative assessments are rarely terminal; we have to make a decision, take a course of action and, in so doing, use self-assessment and the advice and assessments of others, if available. We then use the evidence for that decision, formatively, as a basis for future action. A real world answer to the "when?" question must be that self-assessment data is potentially of great value at all times. It seems that different opinions about the use of self-assessment data in summative documents are based on varying interpretations of the purpose of those documents. For example, de Groot, writing in Broadfoot (1986), emphasises that

> "It is neither desirable nor practicable to divorce the formative from any proposed summative process. . . . The differences between personal recording and records of achievement represent an immediate challenge, yet they are not irreconcilable."

How Can Self-Assessment Contribute Effectively?

If a student's contribution to an assessment record is to be seen as effective, efforts must be made to achieve accuracy and reliability. This implies consideration of two important questions:

What aspects of an assessment system lend themselves to self-assessment?

How may students be trained to self-assess?

When it comes to assessing characteristics like "confidence" "imagination" and "perseverence", a student's self-assessment is potentially more reliable than any other. One approach could be to use self-assessment data for personal or affective aspects, but otherwise to use external assessment measures. This separation, however, is unnecessarily simplistic.

The evidence from the studies of Cowan (1975) and Burke (1969) suggests that although students are not good at accurate self-assessment of their work when they have to try to determine the criteria for themselves, when the criteria for assessment are clearly established and understood by students, the reliability of their self-assessments improves. It would make little sense, of course, to ask students to record a self-assessment on an aspect for which external "objective" assessment is available (e.g. a summative record of "O" Grade or "O" level achievement), but students *can* be trained to self-assess performance in a system where the learning outcomes and assessment criteria are clearly laid down. This is the basis for much of the learning within the modular programme of the National Certificate at 16 + in Scotland. Even within the university system where assessment criteria may be less easy to identify, Cowan has found that it is possible to establish a programme helping students to reflect on their learning and assess it more accurately. A judicious combination of self-assessment and peer-assessment will often produce more reliable results than self-assessment alone. Peer-assessment may be of particular value in helping to clarify ideas and, at the same time, providing the teacher with useful diagnostic information, especially in aesthetic subjects. The value of self- and peer-assessment, however, may not be immediately apparent to students, especially if the criteria for assessment have been laid down by teachers or others. They will have to be given adequate time and support, therefore, to learn to use self-assessment formatively, so that its benefit becomes apparent. Only then will they be motivated to carry out such assessments carefully and accurately.

Other issues to consider when examining how student self-assessment may be most effective are those of deciding which aspects of the learning and experiences will be assessed, who will enter up the assessments, and the value of pupil-teacher negotiation in the assessment process. Burgess and Adams (1980, 1986) argue that these three issues dealt with together can produce an assessment which involves students in both formative and summative records. Student and teacher enter into a dialogue, reviewing the student's progress and jointly agreeing on targets to be achieved. A summative document would then comprise statements about the student's experience and achievements, chosen by the student after discussion with the teacher. This type of approach is seen as the basis for a whole new learning relationship between teachers and students with shared control based on partnership rather than teacher domination. However, a move towards shared control could imply that students would have the power to evaluate the curriculum and teaching as well as themselves, and to expect changes to be made in response to their feedback.

The Fife Profile

In beginning to set up a system of profiling within the Fife scheme, the TVEI team had some of the issues described in this paper at the front of their minds, but others emerged as the process developed. It is important to remember that profiling in Scotland is not, and should not, be considered as exclusive to TVEI. Furthermore, TVEI is not intended as a new subject or as an add-on to the present curriculum. Rather TVEI should be seen as offering new curriculum opportunities, across all subjects. Thus the profiling system implemented in Fife has originated within the TVEI

Project but is designed to be able to be used, across the curriculum, in any school.

The original agreement with the Manpower Services Commission (MSC) committed the Fife TVEI team to:

develop a recording and reviewing system, including a weekly log, which would allow students to record experiences and achievements;

offer appropriate opportunities for students to develop their personal and social skills;

establish competence-based assessment procedures leading to a summative profile.

The Process

The profiling process designed to meet these aims is now in its third year and covers the third to the fifth years of secondary school (S3 to S5) with an introduction through vocational guidance in the second year (S2). The key aspects of this process are shown in Figure 1. Students are encouraged to compile formative records from which a selection can be made to produce a summative profile. The process covers the students' activities in the classroom, in work experience placements, and in activities such as visits and community work; it relates, in fact, to *all* situations in which a TVEI student may find him or herself. It aims to integrate the recording and reviewing process with the curriculum and offer each student the opportunity to collate a description of his or her experiences and progress on a weekly basis. A typical third and fourth year student Log Sheet is shown in Figure 2. At the end of each TVEI unit of work (ten weeks in S3 and 8 in S4), the student completes a Review Sheet (see Figure 3).

The Log Sheets and Review Sheets thus form the main vehicle for the formative assessment record completed by the student from fourteen to sixteen years of age. To these are added the records of work experience placements

THE PROFILING PROCESS
KEY ASPECTS OF PERSONAL, SOCIAL AND VOCATIONAL EDUCATION IN TVEI (FIFE) PILOT

FIGURE 1

Recording and Reviewing comprises a weekly log of experience and achievements, progress in personal and core learning skills development, and records of work and related experiences (across all units of work).

S2 *Vocational Guidance*	S3	S4 *Vocational Guidance*	S5
PREPARATION FOR SUBJECT CHOICE	Recording and Reviewing	Recording And Reviewing	LIVE AND LEARN
Self Awareness	Preparation and Choices For	Profiling And The Profile	Learning and How to Learn
Decision Making	*AWARE 1. (3 days)	Equal Opportunities	Recording and Reviewing
Problem Solving Approach	Briefing for AWARE 1	Self Awareness	Learning Strategy
Learning	AWARE 1 – Work Based	Occupational Awareness	Understanding Roles
Local Job Opportunities	Projects	Alternative Routes	Personal, Social, Educational
Sex Stereotyping	Debrief of AWARE 1	Other Alternatives, e.g.	and Vocational Needs
Recording and Reviewing		Unemployment	
Summary Profile	YOU AND INDUSTRY	Decisions Making	Individual/Group Study
	(10 week unit)	Transition	
			Selection of Case Studies
	JOB PROFILE based on	Preparation and Choices for	exemplifying roles of a variety
S2 JIIG CAL	Job Families	AWARE 2 (5 days)	of people and how they are
	Core Skills	Briefing for AWARE 2	affected by Social Needs,
	Industrial Visits	AWARE 2 – Job Study	including Health and Fitness,
	Questionnaires	Debrief of AWARE 2	Budgeting, Consumer Rights.
	Individual & Group Reviews		Assessing individual needs
			now and in the near future.
			Survey of Needs for Aware 3.
			Preparation for AWARE 3.
			AWARE 3 – to suit individual
			needs (up to 10 days)
			Debrief of Aware 3.
FOLIO of key examples of Learning experiences	FOLIO of key examples of Learning experiences	FOLIO of key examples of Learning experiences	FOLIO of key examples of Learning experiences
		SUMMARY PROFILE	*PROFILE UPDATE*

*AWARE = Awareness of Work and Related Experiences – structured work experience programme.

FIGURE 2

RECORDING AND REVIEWING
LOG SHEET

Name: .... **Class**........

School: ....

Now that you have found out how to complete your log sheet fill in this sample for the work you have done today.

GENERAL QUESTIONS

What should you have achieved in TVEI work this week?

Was there any part of the work you did not achieve?

Why?

What will you do about this?

CORE SKILLS

Which core skills did you practise – in TVEI work?
 Problem Solving:
 Practical:
 Number:
 Communication:

– in school or elsewhere this week?
 Problem Solving:
 Practical:
 Number:
 Communication:

YOUR COMMENTS

Comments about this week's TVEI work (e.g. were any parts useful/interesting/ a waste of time?) *Explain why*.

Pupil's Signature:..

Teacher's Signature:..

FIGURE 3

UNIT TITLE: **RECORDING AND REVIEWING**

REVIEW

Name: .... **Class**........

School: ....

At the end of each unit you should complete a REVIEW SHEET. This will give you an opportunity to look back and think about the work you have done.

Which part(s) of the unit did you find most interesting?

Why did you find it interesting? e.g. "because you enjoy working in groups".

Is there any part(s) of the work done in this unit you would like to know more about? If so, which part(s)?

Is there any part(s) of the unit you did not find interesting? If so, which part(s)?

How does the work on this TVEI unit fit in with the other work you have done in school.

Has recording and reviewing the Core Skills helped to make you more aware of your own skills?

Which skills do you think might be *most* useful to you in the future?

Pupil's Signature:...

Teacher's Signature:...

(Work Based Projects and Log Books), vocational guidance activities and the completion of Job Profiles as part of a *You and Industry* unit. Information from all these experiences is gathered and processed by students. Decisions about what to enter onto any recording sheet are the student's. A timetable period is allocated each week for this recording and reviewing process and a tutor is available to discuss entries and to countersign each sheet, indicating his or her acceptance of the accuracy of the comments recorded. A particular emphasis in the recording and reviewing process is put on Core Skills (skills which are common to many tasks and essential for the successful completion of most tasks) and a separate cumulative Review Sheet for core skills is also completed at the end of each unit. Students are additionally encouraged, at the end of Unit Review, to consider how TVEI work has related to other curricular activities.

The Summary Profile

The first Summary Profile is produced at the end of S4 and is described as "a pupil's *self*-portrait in relation to interests, abilities, relationships, skills and experiences". The first two pages of the summative profile are represented by Figure 4. The third page consists of a list of qualifications and other experiences to be entered by the pupil. The completed profile is the property of the student and copies can only be distributed to school, TVEI centre, and parents if the student wishes. The profile is signed by a tutor to attest to its accuracy, but there is presently no section for any comments from teachers or others. (Employers can record comments in the placement logbooks and Work-Based Projects if the student asks them to do so.)

In making their entries, students are encouraged by tutors to refer to records of key learning experiences which they have extracted over two years to form folios. The compilation of folios usually involves a good deal of

FIGURE 4

LIST OF CATEGORIES IN THE SUMMATIVE PROFILE OF FIFE TVEI

STUDENT PROFILE: PERSONAL INTERESTS

— HOW I SEE MYSELF NOW

— QUALITIES, ABILITIES, RELATIONSHIPS
(Delete words which do not apply to you)

—

Friendly	Observant	Imaginative
Punctual	Caring	Sociable
Adaptable	Organised	Tolerant
Persevering	Ambitious	Hardworking
Creative	Sporting	Understanding
Tidy	Carefree	Courteous
Confident	Even-tempered	Energetic
Quiet	Independent	Patient
Dependable	Coopertive	Attentive

— MY OTHER COMMENTS

— INTERESTS/HOBBIES

— SKILLS I HAVE PRACTISED

— HOW I WOULD LIKE TO PROGRESS
(QUALITIES, INTERESTS, EXPERIENCES)

STUDENT PROFILE: VOCATIONAL INTERESTS

— EXPERIENCES OF WORKING LIFE

— JOB INTERESTS

JOB FAMILY (OTF)   TYPE OF JOB/S   TYPE OF FIRM

— SKILLS I WOULD LIKE TO DEVELOP

— HOW I WOULD LIKE TO PROGRESS AT WORK

student-teacher dialogue and this carries forward to the crucial process of drawing up a final portfolio of examples to back up the statements in the Summary Profile. The support of the tutor is essential at this stage. The summative profile is then updated at the end of S5 with evidence for the update gathered from a more flexible four-weekly recording and reviewing sheet linked to a unit called *Live and Learn* which encourages peer- as well as self-assessment. In S5 particular emphasis is put on the role of the tutor as someone who is available to support *if* and *when* asked.

It is not possible, in a chapter of this length, to adequately summarise three years of work by an enthusiastic and committed TVEI scheme; but, given this brief outline, how do the reactions to this approach to student self-assessment relate to the three key aspects considered initially

why should the student self-assess?

when can self-assessment be most useful?

how can self-assessment contribute effectively?

Why?

The following comments about the profiling process come from a group of students who began TVEI in 1984:

"The review was useful in getting me to reflect on my learning—it helped with physics."

"Recording and reviewing could be useful to help locate mistakes."

"It helped looking forward and back in thinking about what you would do next week."

"I don't want the teachers to take over and tell me what to put in my recording and reviewing."

"It makes pupils more aware of the teacher's role."

"I found the personal qualities bits very helpful because I didn't think about myself like that before."

"I asked the teacher and other pupils what they thought about the meaning of words like was I tolerant?"

"I thought that the work based projects were useful for recording things—it's good to know what the employer thought."

"It wasn't too good to begin with because I think you need someone to put pressure on you—otherwise you see things as a skive."

These responses provide some support for the arguments advanced as to why students should be encouraged to self-assess. On the topic of student-teacher communication, the following comments were made by two TVEI tutors:

"It tends to encourage pupils to open up more and be more realistic."

"The pupil-teacher dialogue gives it more credibility."

"It makes the whole learning situation easier. I've found out things I never knew about pupils—especially what they do outside school."

"It needs working on by teachers so that they are all speaking with one voice."

"It helps the pupils to set goals for their personal benefit."

"I was surprised that pupils tend more often to under-estimate themselves than overestimate."

When?

With respect to the question of *when* students might usefully self-assess, the Fife TVEI team have committed themselves to a system which is based on self-assessment at both formative and summative stages. The link between formative and summative is that *the student alone completes both*. This does not reflect Rowntree's idea that a summative document should include comments from teachers and others. However, the Fife Profile was introduced in the middle of an industrial dispute, when it was unlikely that teachers would be prepared to become fully involved in the TVEI scheme and its associated assessment. It is intended that future summative profile documents will contain a section which can be completed by a teacher, but at the request of the student.

The audience for the Fife Profile is primarily the student, but credibility for the summative profile is presently being sought with local employers and colleges. It is being recommended to this audience as a useful basis for an interview, but there is a long way to go in dealing with objections of the type identified by one student:

> "I think it's good—but employers don't recognise it—all they want to know is how many 'O' grades you've got—and if you fill it all in they might think you're lying."

How?

The model for the profiling process adopted by Fife probably has most in common with the proposals of Burgess and Adams and the work of Hitchcock in Avon, particularly with reference to *how* self-assessment may most effectively be used. Although all the recording of assessment is carried out by students, entries are often discussed with a tutor and other students. In S5 in particular, emphasis is put on establishing targets and plans as well as reviewing progress and these targets are usually negotiated with a tutor. Peer-assessment is also encouraged in S5, and there is a section for tutor comments. Students can record their academic achievements on the Profile, but they are not encouraged to compile self-assessment comments on aspects for which external certification is available. However, the Fife Profile does not enter as far into the formative process as Burgess and Adams would wish in offering students "opportunities to criticise the teaching and the curriculum they already receive, and to negotiate changes in it where appropriate" as a result of their self-assessment data. Students have choices between different options in selecting TVEI experiences. They can also negotiate personal targets when carrying out TVEI activities, but it is not really possible for student self-assessment to allow negotiation of different curricular objectives for that individual. Rather the results of student self-assessments are used as "course" or "unit" evaluation information when TVEI staff are considering revisions of that element for the next year group. Student-teacher communication is certainly encouraged within this profiling system, but the communication is more often in the form of discussion of experiences than negotiation of the curriculum, particularly in S3 and S4.

The reliance on self-assessment in the Fife profiling process is not a serious problem with respect to accuracy, since the "headings" used for self-assessment comments are confined mainly to descriptions of personal qualities, experiences and progress, and these are areas where, if anything, evidence suggests that self-assessors under-estimate themselves. Peer-assessment is not widely advocated until S5 and is usually used in non-academic areas of activity. An interesting example of peer-assessment being used within the subject of English is to be found in Hawick High School, which is involved in the Borders TVEI scheme. Martin Morini, the Principal Teacher, has set up a system which allows a small group of students to discuss and negotiate a marking scheme for a piece of work and then to set and mark that piece of work for the rest of the class, providing feedback to justify the assessments made. Another interesting method of peer-assessment is practised by Alan Beattie, Principal Teacher of Music at

Keith Grammar School. He encourages pupils to request assessment from peers and the teacher "when they feel ready for it" and asks them to assess each other's work on aspects of composition such as "impact". It is particularly useful to invoke self- and peer-assessment of this type in aesthetic subject areas, where standards are less objective and there may be considerable variance between a teacher's view of an acceptable standard and that of students. Peer-assessment can provide teachers with valuable insights into the value systems of students.

Profiles and Control

The introduction of student self-assessment is frequently claimed to lead to the student having control over what is to be learned. Several writers (e.g. Hargreaves, 1986; Stronach, 1986), however, have argued that self-assessment may lead to "pupil-focussed confessions" rather than "learner-centred dialogues", and that records of achievement may fulfil purposes of external selection and surveillance rather than of promoting student motivation and independence. With these potential dangers in mind, how does the Fife Profiling System rate in terms of relinquishing some control of the system to students?

In the Summary Profile, the list of qualities, abilities and relationships against which a student is asked to compare him or herself, has not been selected by that student, nor even by that year group of students. It is a list drawn up after careful consultation with industry and other interested parties, and containing items contributed by training managers in industry. Furthermore, it requires students to delete what does not apply to them without them being able to add, in that section, words that they do feel apply to them. As one student said:

> "I crossed out quiet, 'cos I don't think it's good to be very quiet, but I'd liked to have had talkative on the list."

Students can add qualities in the "other comments" section, but they are seen as being "less important" than the first list. This section fails the test of being a student-centred self-portrait; it is, instead, student-focussed "painting by numbers". The terms used, apart from being chosen by others, having little meaning for the student as they are presented on the Profile. They may be backed up by portfolio examples of experiences when these properties were demonstrated, but the distillation from the contextualised portfolio examples to the summative profile can result in a loss of meaning which is misleading to both the student and any other audience for the profile.

In other respects the Fife Profile tries to ensure ipsative rather than normative recording by providing students with a completed exemplar profile which avoids the use of normative referents like "as good as", "could be better than" and "nearly up to . . .". The category headings for the Profile relate to the formative records, but where chosen without reference to the students. One student commented:

> "Many of the headings are not much use. I like the first one on 'progress' but after that they get repetitive and you end up putting the same thing down again."

More discussion with a tutor would undoubtedly ensure that a student completed the form in the way the designers intended, but perhaps a better solution would be to have more student involvement in establishing the headings for recording summative profile comments? A case for the student-teacher dialogue to be negotiation rather than discussion?

It is nevertheless easy to be critical of an assessment system which, by the very nature of TVEI, had to be thought up and implemented within six months. The Fife Profiling approach is firmly committed to student self-assessment and is making a serious attempt to involve students in both the formative and summative processes. It is not yet the case that students genuinely "take control" of their own assessment but it is moving in the direction of "done by" rather than "done to" student assessment. It will be interesting to see how the system is modified during the remaining two years of the TVEI pilot and with the implementation of TVEI extension.

Acknowledgement

Special thanks are due to the Fife TVEI project team, particularly Katherine Russell, Margaret Stewart and Fiona Shearer for their help in the preparation of this chapter.

REFERENCES

Burke, R. J. (1969). "Some preliminary data on the use of self-evaluation and the use of peer-ratings in assigning university course grades", *Journal of Educational Research*, 62 (10), 444–448.
Burgess, T. and Adams, E. (1980). *Outcomes of Education*, London: Macmillan.
Burgess, T. and Adams, E. (1986). "Records for all at 16", in Broadfoot, P. (ed.), *Profiles and Records of Achievement—A Review of Issues and Practice*, London: Holt, Rinehart and Winston.
Cowan, J. (1975). "The ability to appraise one's own work", *Higher Education Bulletin*, 3 (2), 127–128.
De Groot, R. (1986). "Pupils Personal Records", in Broadfoot, P. (ed.), *Profiles and Records of Achievement—A Review of Issues and Practice*, London: Holt, Rinehart and Winston.
Hargreaves, A. (1986). "Ideological records breakers?", in Broadfoot, P. (ed.), *Profiles and Records of Achievement—A Review of Issues and Practice*, London: Holt, Rinehart and Winston.
Hitchcock, G. (1986). *Profiles and Profiling—A Practical Introduction*, Harlow: Longman.
Rowntree, D. (1987). *Assessing Students: How Shall We Know Them?*, London: Kogan Page.
Scottish Council for Research in Education (1977). *Pupils in Profile*, London: Hodder and Stoughton.
Stansbury, D. (1974). *Record of Personal Experience*, South Brent, Devon: RPE Publications.

CHAPTER 5

PROFILES AND RECORDS OF ACHIEVEMENT

Sally Brown and Harry Black

The Scottish Council for Research in Education

Introduction

There is a growing interest and literature in the field of profiles and records of achievement (ROA). Not only are there now a variety of books available (e.g. Broadfoot, 1986 and 1987; Hitchcock, 1986; Law, 1984) which provide excellent accounts of theory and practice in the field, but also there are clear policy initiatives on the development of ROAs from the Manpower Services Commission (MSC), in relation to the Technical and Vocational Education Initiative (TVEI), and the Department of Education and Science (DES and the Welsh Office, 1984).

In this chapter we will concentrate on a broad introduction to ROAs, and will make no attempt to make subtle distinctions between the concepts of the "profile" and of the "ROA": the terms will be used interchangeably. Our concern is with the general nature of ROAs; the reasons for, and history of, the growth of interest in them; the ways in which they are starting to be implemented in schools; the problems for, and impact on, schools associated with that implementation; and an identification of some of the questions which remain to be answered in this field.

What is a Record of Achievement?

At one level, ROAs may be seen as extended documents which incorporate explicit statements about a range of achievements or experiences going well beyond the single assessments in traditional subjects. They will have several elements which may relate to affective or cognitive characteristics of pupils, assessments in non-traditional areas of the curriculum (e.g. work experience), assessments made by a variety of assessors (including pupils) and curricula which may be common across schools (e.g. GCSE) or specific to one class.

An effective ROA is expected to make clear what achievements each of its elements refers to and the context in which those achievements have been assessed. It should identify, therefore, not only the skills, knowledge, personal qualities or other pupil competencies of concern, but also the courses, activities, topics and environments in which the assessments were made. It is also necessary to enable the reader to understand the basis on which judgements have been made about the levels of performance or qualities of the achievements. The extent of detail provided will depend on who the reader is and the purpose for which the ROA is to be used.

An ROA, therefore, is a means of presenting a collection of assessments, but it does *not*, in principle, imply

  (i)   that any particular means of assessment is used
 (ii)   that any particular person or agency is responsible for making the assessments (e.g. teacher, work experience employer, pupil, examination board)
(iii)   that the assessment should be used only for summative or only for formative purposes
 (iv)   that the assessments should be internal rather than external to the school or college
  (v)   that the assessments should take one specific form (e.g. marks, grades, comments, mastery/non-mastery decisions)

(vi) that the form of ROAs should be identical across classes/schools

(vii) that the assessments are criterion-referenced rather than norm-referenced

(viii) that the same amount or type of information has to be supplied for each element of the ROA

(ix) that the same amount or type of information on the various elements has to be provided for all users (e.g. parents, employers, tertiary education).

The notion of ROAs described above would be criticised by many people as essentially static. That is, it puts far too much emphasis on the document itself and not nearly enough on the *process* of constructing the record. This process is frequently seen as the most crucial element and much of the current literature on ROAs is concerned with just that. Indeed, some schemes are toying with the idea of not producing a summative document at all or, at most, see such a document as of marginal importance compared to the impact of ROAs on the teaching/learning relationship itself. Because Chapter 4 looks in some depth at the process involved in profiling and in the production of ROAs, it was decided that the emphasis in this chapter would be rather different. Although we are not limiting ourselves to consideration of only those ROAs which are used as summative reports of achievement, we are concerned primarily with circumstances in which some form of document is produced, whether for formative or summative purposes.

However one chooses to answer the question "What is a Record of Achievement?", there is clearly considerable scope for variation in the nature and form of ROAs. But what are the justifications made for changing from comfortable traditional modes of assessment into a new and relatively uncharted area?

What are the Reasons for the Growth of Interest in ROAs?

Much of the early impetus in the United Kingdom arose from substantial concern that large numbers of young people were ill-served by the conventional examination. The grades of the Scottish Certificate of Education and the General Certificate of Education, university classes of degrees, grading in teacher education and marks in school examinations, it was said, indicated little about what had been learned. Many young people received no certificates, and those who did had little more than a measure of how much better or worse their performance was than the average for their group. Furthermore, this kind of assessment system was seen as having a constraining effect on the curriculum, by narrowing it down to what could be assessed through traditional examining techniques. Broader curricula and other achievements, it was suggested, went unrewarded.

Many people felt assessment should include other competences and qualities which cannot be assessed by traditional examinations. If the curriculum stresses the importance of pupils' attitudes, initiative, problem-solving capabilities, competence in social interaction and respect for society, then why are those qualities not included in the assessments? If pupils' personal qualities are the area in which employers are interested, then why do they not have a place on the report of achievement? If traditional examining methods rely on inscriptive techniques, then how do we take account of the fact that many people reveal qualities of creativity, fluency, imagination, reasoning, drive and persistence through modes of expression other than inscriptive forms? (Stevenson, 1983, quoting Rowntree, 1977).

A second major concern has been to introduce a system in which pupils are involved with the teacher in the assessment process. This is seen as leading to greater pupil understanding of the meaning of the assessments, the assessment having a motivating effect and the pupils making use of assessment for their own purposes. The importance of including pupils' self-asessments and arranging opportunities for teachers and pupils to negotiate the contents of the ROAs is frequently stressed. Much is made of the ROA "belonging to the pupil", and teachers are encouraged to discuss with pupils the kind of achievements which the records will report and the evidence which will be used in formulating the assessments. In this way, it is argued, pupils will develop an awareness of how the assessments relate to the curriculum they are offered and how the judgements made about them are (or are not) based on the evidence.

It is also suggested that the broader and detailed ROAs will be more effective than traditional assessments in encouraging teachers to examine their curriculum intentions closely and discuss their teaching and assessments with colleagues. Not only are ROAs seen as reminders about the curriculum to be covered and evidence to be collected, they are also regarded as a check on whether educational goals are over-ambitious or over-modest. In other words, they have the potential to contribute to the evaluation of strengths and weaknesses in courses or teaching.

The most direct justification for the worth of ROAs to teachers, however, points to their value in diagnosing pupils' strengths and weaknesses and guiding decisions about counselling individuals. In addition, teachers are seen as being in a position to offer "outsiders" more informative accounts of pupils over a range of achievements. An obvious gain here, for ROAs over traditional assessments, is the reduction in pressure to aggregate assessments across various achievements which may be quite different in nature. In theory, therefore, ROAs retain the meaningful information which is lost by reporting as single grades or marks.

There is a general feeling that ROAs can make the curriculum-assessment link much stronger. A corollary of that follows which suggests that control or standardisation of curricula in schools, colleges or youth training could be made more effective by the introduction of ROAs. Whether that is an attractive argument depends on whether one is likely to be the controller or the controlled.

What is the Genesis of Records of Achievement in Scotland and in England and Wales?

The notion of providing a description of strengths and weaknesses has roots in higher education, notably in the Antipodes and the United States, where job applications are often accompanied by a "testimony" which describes much more than an honours classification. As a descriptive account of pupil progress, there are roots in the extensive written reports from some schools, particularly in the private sector and in England and Wales. However, it was substantial Scottish interest in profiling in the 1970s which spurred much of the present development. The Head-teachers' Association of Scotland initiative in 1972 led to the Scottish Council for Research in Education (SCRE) *Pupils in Profile* project (SCRE, 1977) which looked at a form of reporting attainment over a wide range of competencies applicable to the whole age cohort, and not just to those who traditionally succeeded in external examinations. Subsequently, the Dunning Committee's Report (Scottish Education Department, 1977) and its recommendations on "Certificates for All" rather took the wind from the sails of Scottish profiling. There was some impact on, for example, the Clydebank EEC Project, and the (unpublished) SCRE Survey of School Reporting indicated that it had more influence on school reporting than did external certification. However, the greatest thrust in assessment in the 1980s has been towards alternative forms of external certification rather than profiling.

There are two threads to the growth of interest in England and Wales. One of these arose from an interest in the Scottish approach, and the support of SCRE was requested for a number of initiatives. The most elaborate of these was the "City and Guilds" summative profile, but the late seventies and early eighties saw many schemes based on the Scottish model.

The other thread is more clearly English in origin. In Swindon and later in Devon, Stansbury (1974, 1977 and 1984) developed and promoted first a "Record of Personal Achievement" and later a "Record of Personal Experience, Qualities and Qualifications". These comprised extensive pupil-compiled documents. They mapped the wide range of experiences which the young person had found to be of interest in his or her formal and informal learning, were negotiated with teachers and, in some cases, comprised many pages of pupil-written account. The young person could then present this to a prospective employer and thus provide a broader base on which to make decisions than the traditional examination grades. There were problems, not only because of the demanding regulations on how they should be compiled, but also because the potential value to users was questioned. Nevertheless, by the early eighties a number of vociferous pressure groups (see Burgess and Adams, 1980) had been persuaded by what they saw as the pedagogic potential of such an approach.

The growing interest in profiling and records of achievement in England and Wales, in parallel with a virtual dearth of development in Scotland in the eighties, can probably be explained by the inverse rate of change in external certification. In England and Wales the focus was on the changes needed to rationalise an unwieldy number of General Certificate of Education and Certificate of Secondary Education Examination Boards. With its single examination board, Scotland was better placed to concentrate on the rapid development and implementation of new systems for certification: Scottish Certificate of Education Standard Grade (see Chapter 6) and the National

Certificate (see Chapter 7). With this preoccupation, and despite our early initiation through *Pupils in Profile*, we appear to have no national position either for or against the development of ROAs.

What is the Nature of ROAs in Schools?

Among the large number of ROAs being developed and tested in schools in England and Wales, there are nine pilot schemes funded, from 1985 to 1988, by the DES. The progress of these schemes, based in single local education authorities or multi-authority consortia, is being evaluated by researchers from the University of Bristol and the Open University. The team (Patricia Broadfoot, Desmond Nuttal, Mary James, Barry Stierer and Sue Meeking) have some preliminary findings which they have described (private communication) as

". . . early, provisional, descriptive and impressionistic and should on no account be taken to represent either an 'emerging view' on our part or on the part of the DES, or a prescription directed at schools".

These findings however, are the best evidence available about the variation among schools in the nature of ROAs, and we wish to express our thanks to the evaluation team for keeping us informed through their written reports. They suggest that this variation can best be described in terms of five interrelated dimensions.

First, there is a distinction between *pastoral* and *academic* elements of ROAs. The *pastoral* reflects the school's work in areas like social education, health education and pupil guidance activities. Such pastoral schemes emphasise pupil self-recording, diary-keeping, review questions and pupil-teacher interviews. Decisions to concentrate ROAs on the pastoral may arise from emphasis the school places on such things as social education; alternatively, they may reflect a reluctance by high-status academic departments to change their traditional assessment procedures.

ROAs emphasising the *academic* element place importance on recording achievements in specific subject areas and some cross-curricular achievements. Such schemes may well occur in schools which put major emphasis on academic achievements and where staff regard themselves as primarily subject specialists. But academic ROAs also seem likely to occur in schools where the academic departments have some freedom in designing their own assessment records, rather than having to conform to some school profile. The evaluators report that most schools manage to include subject achievement, cross-curricular skills and personal experience in some way in their ROAs.

The second dimension relates to whether the ROA is a *whole school* scheme or is manifest as *departmental* developments. The former tend to be pastoral (personal and cross-curricular skills) and the latter academic.

A third source of variation concerns whether the ROA is in the form of a *package* developed outside, but adopted by, the school. Some teachers welcome a coherent package which they can implement and adapt in minor ways to their own needs. In other cases a more *organic* development, where teachers generate their own scheme based on their own principles and practices, is preferred.

The fourth dimension refers to the extent to which each element of the ROA is structured. The elements may be *criteria-led* with "criteria" consisting of highly structured banks of statements or comments from which a choice is made as an appropriate assessment for an individual pupil on that element. These kinds of criteria facilitate a uniformity of approach among teachers, but many find them constraining. Alternatively, the "criteria" may be identified only as fairly general principles for making the assessments. The latter represents a move towards the *open-ended* end of the continuum. While this open-ended approach, in principle, should enable a more valid and informative record to be generated for each pupil, some teachers report that it encourages aimlessness in teacher-pupil discussions.

And fifthly, schools' projects vary in their emphasis on *formative* or *summative* functions of ROAs. So far, the bulk of efforts have been put into assessment for formative purposes, and the teachers agree the process must start early if pupils are to learn and make effective use of such procedures as self-assessment and assessment review. Among the matters to be resolved in this area, however, are the questions of how to keep the data down to a manageable size, and what relationships there should be between the formative and summative procedures. Should negative assessments of pupils be eschewed in the formative as well as the summative ROA? Can formative reports be used as interim summative reports? Are teachers justified in feeling uneasy in their expectation that summative "user-oriented" products will impose constraints on the processes they are developing for formative use?

What are the Problems For, and Impact On, Schools Introducing ROAs?

The vision of the "ideal" ROA has been concerned with something on which pupil and teacher collaborate and negotiate to produce a record belonging to the pupil. That record would be concerned with a wide range of pupils' qualities, reported in a positive way and according him or her recognition, status and privacy. But is it feasible to relinquish the old model of the teacher as "the assessor" and the pupil "the assessed"? Can the reviewing procedures of ROA schemes ensure both valid assessments and democratic negotiation? Will pupils feel a sense of control of their own destiny, a guarantee of privacy, an assurance that they will know who has access to their records?

From the teachers' perspective, there have been the familiar problems of identifying elements and criteria for assessment. In subject-specific contexts should the elements and criteria be comparable across classes and schools, or should they be relatively open-ended and reflect the particular curriculum followed? In contexts where cross-curricular skills and concepts have been the concern, the fostering of cross-curricular approaches has not easily been achieved. There are still serious questions about the skills' and concepts' generalisability, and the criteria are difficult to apply in comparable ways across the curriculum. This has led to little uniformity among teachers within the same ROA scheme, and schools seem unable to find time for teachers to meet together to develop strategies to overcome this kind of problem.

Time, always a crucial concern, is needed to develop the ROA scheme, for face-to-face discussions with pupils about the assessments, and to prepare the actual reports. Can teachers be given additional "free" time for these tasks? How often should reviews of ROAs with pupils be carried out? How should the curriculum and timetable be adjusted to accommodate such reviews? Are staff prepared for a reduction in time for subject teaching? Can time and resources be found for in-service training for teachers to acquire skills such as those of face-to-face interviewing and complex profiled assessment? Can local authorities provide sufficient and qualified supply cover to release teachers for ROA-related activities? Would it be better to use money for such cover or, instead, to pay teachers to attend courses outside school hours and so avoid disruption caused by substitute teaching?

An important feature of ROAs has been the interviews and discussions between teachers and pupils to review assessments. Teachers and pupils alike see them as being of considerable value, but they are time consuming, often have to be carried out in normal class time, depend on the skills of the teacher and the maturity of the pupil, and frequently do not entail the negotiation about the assessment which was intended. Not only do most teachers have to acquire new skills, they also have to consider the extent to which they can guide, intervene, interfere or refuse to discuss with pupils the content, format and quality of ROAs. What does it mean to say that an ROA "belongs to the young person"?

The area where pupils' self-assessment may be most appropriate is their own personal qualities. The problems posed in conceptualising those qualities, finding valid assessment techniques and justifying the inclusion of such assessments (made in school but "used" in other contexts where their validity is suspect) are daunting.

In relation to personal qualities, the inclusion of negative assessments is difficult. In general, the DES has discouraged the use of negative statements. Some teachers have seen this as dishonest and argue that employers will always read between the lines.

There is also concern that profiling and the tutorial or discussion activities are intruding on pupils' privacy. When asked to talk and write about personal thoughts and feelings in unfamiliar ways, young people may react by producing what they think the teacher wants. Efforts have to be made to develop codes of ethics for interviews and, for example, pupils' diaries. Furthermore, the confidentiality and access to records are still moot points. Given these uncertainties, it is not surprising that teachers report some lack of enthusiasm for ROAs on the part of pupils. On the other hand, pupils gave largely positive responses to a direct question on this from the evaluators.

As with many innovations, the appointment of an ROA co-ordinator for the school turns out to have significance, and most appointments have worked out well. There seem to have been two approaches. In the first, a member of the school's senior management has been co-ordinator; the senior involvement is seen as giving the project credibility throughout the school. In some cases, however, the senior person has been regarded as remote from direct experience of the ROA. The second approach, has involved appointing someone associated directly in the ROA work. This is justified by arguing that such a development should be teacher-led and not imposed by senior management. There is a danger, however, that someone too far down the school hierarchy, and lacking the authority to stimulate others to undertake the developments, may be appointed.

The enthusiasm of staff ranges from "passionate pioneering" to "apathy and outright hostility" (particularly where the ROA scheme is associated with activities or departments held in low esteem by the staff). Reactions may relate to schools' abilities to set up structures and mechanisms to support and evaluate the project; the national teachers' disputes of recent years have restricted meetings of project teams, and made for minimal contact between the co-ordinator and other teachers involved. In general, communications within schools have been a considerable problem in circumstances where only certain teachers and target groups of pupils were involved in the developments.

As yet, there is scant evidence for the impact of the ROA schemes on schools' curricula, existing assessment and reporting systems and administrative organisations. There are, however, indications that ROAs have been accompanied by changes to modular or integrated approaches, adjustment in the balance of pastoral and academic teaching to match the balance of the ROA assessment, movement towards ROAs to complement (or replace) traditional reports to parents, and some examples of school managements putting more emphasis on their pastoral programme, cross-curricular approaches and general support for profiling.

But what of liaison on ROAs between the secondary schools and feeder primaries, the LEA pilot scheme as a whole, employers, tertiary courses and parents? Progress on this front has been slow because priority has been given to the development of ROAs. Only rarely have primary schools developed ROA-related methods to ease transfer to secondary school. Problems are apparent also at points of transfer to upper schools and colleges; there is little chance for pupils to build on their ROA experiences, and transfer to other profile assessments (e.g. City and Guilds of London Institute, Certificate of Pre-Vocational Education, Royal Society of Arts) is not without difficulties.

Where parents have engaged in the developments, they have been enthusiastic. They have shown concern, however, where banks of comments have been used rather than open-ended approaches, and in cases where there have been "gaps" in their child's report. Such gaps may mean that the pupil has had little opportunity to develop those qualities, or they may reflect a reluctance to present a negative assessment. The small number of employers who have been consulted have appeared unimpressed by ROAs which contain exclusively positive assessments.

Perhaps the greatest concern is for relationships between the schools and the LEA pilot scheme as a whole. Some relationships are harmonious but there are cases of substantial conflict on the underlying philosophy, approaches, emphases or criteria and the thinking or practices within the school. On past experience, one can speculate that a crucial issue concerns the locus of decision-making. If teachers and schools are expected to shoulder the development work, then they will expect to make the important decisions. Where it appears that "outsiders" can and do override such decisions, a rise in tension (or alternatively a withdrawal of teachers' efforts) is almost inevitable.

What Questions about Records of Achievement Remain to be Answered?

Attractive innovations, which appear to be an improvement on past practice, can develop their own momentum, fueled by enthusiastic supporters. Such popular reforms have to be closely scrutinised. ROAs are no exception and there are still questions about them which have to be answered.

There are technical questions about validity and reliability. The arguments for the validity of ROAs are persuasive. The emphasis on negotiation in ROAs probably achieves high validity in the sense that both young people and teachers see the assessments as having meaning in relation to their personal experience. But this is only one conceptualisation of validity. The evidence on other legitimate interpretations, such as validity as prediction or as an adequate coverage of some domain, is thin. Furthermore, the grounds on which the criteria comprising the profile are selected are seldom spelt out, and there is little hard evidence that the components of most ROAs are sufficiently heterogeneous to justify profiling.

If one is looking at an education system where a summative report is all important, and emphasis is put on making comparisons among individuals' assessment reports, the reliability of ROAs is uncertain and, furthermore, it receives scant attention in the literature (but see Nuttal and Goldstein, 1986). It is extraordinarily difficult to monitor reliability in negotiations among individuals. Since some employers are less than happy about records which report only positive aspects of pupil attainment, and because the public will have to be persuaded that such documents are reliable and useful, effective moderation procedures must be developed to give ROAs the currency they require.

It must be said, however, that where ROA developments are directed towards new learning approaches and teacher-student relationships (rather than towards summative reports), the significance of the traditional reliability concept is less clear. While it is still important that assessments should not provide misleading information, it is the meaning on a personal level which is crucial rather than the reliability (in the sense of accuracy and reproducability).

Given that one argument in favour of ROAs is their potential contribution to teaching and learning, a number of pedagogic questions arise. The England and Wales study is helpful as a general map, but we also need evidence at a more microscopic level. What part do ROAs play in a young person's learning experience? What range of strategies are adopted by teachers and schools and to what extent does each of these realise the hypothesised pedagogic potential? What evidence is there of positive impact in the "normal" classroom context, as opposed to the classroom of the enthusiast? If ROAs become a clerical exercise for some teachers, what might be the consequences?

The use of ROAs also raises psychological questions. The democratic rhetoric suggests they "belong to the pupil", but what does this mean? Could it mean a public display by young people of attitudes and notions which they are *obliged* to reveal? The inclusion of components relating to personal qualities gives rise to moral questions about who should have access to this sort of information. But even if it is restricted to an exercise in "self-awareness", what evidence is there of the impact on young people's development?

There are logistical questions relating to the planning of costs and time. The evidence from the England and Wales study confirms the assumption that this is a time-consuming notion, and that the allocation of responsibility for profiling in the school is crucial. And just as important are the costs to pupils in time which they might otherwise use for alternative learning opportunities. How can the costs in teacher time, allocations of responsibility and pupil time be most effectively managed. These costs need not be seen as additional expense. It may be, for example, that time spent with pupils on ROAs could be a valuable investment of the time already devoted to guidance work; guidance staff, of course, already have responsibility allowances. Nevertheless, it would be naive to assume that ROAs can be implemented nationally without additional resources or the reallocation of responsibility.

This leads inevitably to political questions. In the first place, ROAs are more complex than single global grades, demand more of the reader and do not lend themselves to making easy comparisons among young people. There is contradictory evidence on whether end-users find them worthwhile and whether they adequately represent characteristics in which those users are interested. The relationship between ROAs and traditional examination results remains unclear, but the DES policy statement anticipates their combination into one document. This would imply that the examination boards accept some responsibility for profiling. It is possible, of course, that the introduction of profiles alongside global grades may reveal the arbitrary nature of the aggregation of different assessments to produce single grades, and so trigger public objections to those grades. Alternatively, the profiles may be ignored in favour of the familiar and administratively convenient grade.

If ROAs are to complement, or replace, traditional examination grades on summative certificates, there is the question of when such a certificate should be provided. Should the traditional pattern of a leaving certificate at sixteen be followed? To what extent is sixteen the effective age of entry into employment for young people today? If young people's own experience suggests that these certificates are no longer so important, does this make ROAs at sixteen less relevant because they will have little impact on determining the next stage in the young person's educational or career pattern? Or does it make them more relevant because they could provide a channel out of the external certification rut at that age?

To concentrate on the ROA as a leaving certificate at a particular age, however, may be to distort the whole discussion of a profiling approach. The educational arguments for ROAs do not imply an emphasis on either summative certificates or a particular stage in education. The essential flexibility of the ROA must imply its application to primary, secondary and tertiary education, and in so far as it fulfils a summative function it can (theoretically) be made available when needed.

Acknowledgement

We wish to express our thanks to the evaluation team associated with the DES initiative on ROAs for making available to us some of their early findings and allowing us to use them. This chapter was based on part of a mini-review of work on ROAs which the SED commissioned from SCRE. Any views expressed, however, are those of the authors and are not necessarily shared by either the evaluation team or the SED.

REFERENCES

Broadfoot, P. (ed.) (1986). *Profiles and Records of Achievement*, London: Holt, Rinehart and Winston.

Broadfoot, P. (1987). *Introducing Profiling*, Basingstoke: Macmillan Education Ltd.

Burgess, T. and Adams, E. (1986). *Outcomes of Education*, London: Macmillan.

Department of Education and Science and the Welsh Office (1984). *Records of Achievement: A Statement of Policy*, London: HMSO.

Hitchcock, G. (1986). *Profiles and Profiling: A Practical Introduction*, Harlow: Longmans.

Law, B. (1984). *Uses and Abuses of Profiling*, London: Harper and Row.

Nuttal, D. and Goldstein, H. (1986). "Profiles and Graded Tests: the Technical Issues", in Broadfoot, P. (ed.), *Profiles and Records of Achievement*, London: Holt, Rinehart and Winston.

Rowntree, D. (1977). *Assessing Students: How Shall We Know Them?*, London: Harper and Row.

Scottish Council for Research in Education (1977). *Pupils in Profile: Making the Most of Teacher's Knowledge of Pupils*, London: Hodder and Stoughton.

Scottish Education Department (1977). *Assessment for All: Report of the Committee to Review Assessment in the Third and Fourth Years of Secondary Education in Scotland* ("Dunning Report"), Edinburgh: HMSO.

Stansbury, D. (1974). *Record of Personal Experience*, South Brent, Devon: RPE Publications.

Stansbury, D. (1977). "The case for personal records for every pupil", *Comprehensive Education*, 36, 23–24.

Stansbury, D. (1984). *Principles of Personal Recording*, Totnes, Devon: Springline Trust.

Stevenson, M. (1983). "Pupil profiles—an alternative to conventional examinations?" *British Journal of Educational Studies*, 31 (2), 102–116.

CHAPTER 6

CRITERION REFERENCING AND GRADE RELATED CRITERIA: THE EXPERIENCE OF STANDARD GRADE

Eric Drever
University of Stirling

In 1977 there was published in Scotland the Dunning Report *Assessment For All* (Scottish Education Department, 1977). Although this was primarily concerned with assessment for certification at 16+, it discussed many general issues concerning school assessment. Teachers learned that for years they had been practising something called "norm-referenced assessment" (or NRA) without realising it, and that there was now an alternative on offer, called "criterion-referenced assessment" or CRA. During the massive programme of development and in-service work that followed, the two concepts of NRA and CRA began to take shape in the popular consciousness of the profession.

In our research and in-service work at Stirling we found that teachers thought of criterion-referencing as an approach in which one first defined clearly the standards to be attained, and then assessed whether pupils had attained them. They saw this as having advantages over the traditional norm-referenced system, which aimed mainly to spread out the marks so that pupils could be given different grades. CRA seemed appropriate for curriculum evaluation, for improving teaching, and for helping pupils to learn through "diagnostic tests". Teachers saw it as motivating for the less able pupils, who would no longer get poor grades simply because they were in the lowest ten per cent of the year group, but could now experience success in learning by achieving criteria set at their own level. (See Brown, 1980, for an account of teachers' views.)

However we sensed that in the search for examples of criterion-referenced tests or model programmes of assessment a more fundamental challenge to our thinking was being ignored. It was easy for teachers to recognise deficiencies in traditional examinations: for example, that the usual pass-mark of 50 per cent gave no guarantee that a pupil had mastered the subject, or that a succession of grades of "E" might destroy learners' morale; but they had not necessarily begun to question the principles of NRA, and the assumptions underlying the "numbers game" of marks and grades. Some of the problems that followed stemmed from confusion about these fundamental issues, and it is helpful to consider them at this stage.

Norm-Referenced Assessment: Measuring Ability

The technology of norm-referenced examinations is closely modelled on that of psychological testing. In psychometric work items are generated, vetted and eliminated using procedures very similar to those used by examination boards in developing multiple choice tests using item statistics, and the compelling central concern with statistical reliability and the proper "normal" distribution of scores is the same. But why import this model into education? Psychological tests aim to magnify and extract a measure of some underlying and relatively permanent trait of personality, which is usually supposed to be randomly distributed among the population. Why should this be seen as an appropriate analogy for the process of finding out what each pupil has learned, out of the many things that teachers have been teaching?

One main reason is that our examinations have evolved largely as means of selection, and for that purpose it is seen as necessary to produce a wide spread of scores, and to demonstrate that they are reliable and precise: if 61 per cent gets you into college and 59 per cent does not, then the public will want to know that candidates' scores are *really* different. The norm-referenced model of assessment guarantees that *but only that*. What the numbers *mean*, and wherein the difference lies, are quite another matter.

Another less obvious reason is that examiners may believe that they, like psychologists, are in the "mental measurement" business: not measuring intelligence as such, but something rather similar, namely pupils' "general ability" at a particular subject. If one thinks in this way, then all the various things that pupils have attained in their school work are of interest mainly as evidence of this underlying quality of "ability", which is measured by the total score for the test. Elsewhere I have argued at some length that this notion of "general ability" is not a useful concept (Drever, 1987). It serves to explain away the variation in pupils' attainment by invoking an ill-defined quasi-psychological quality, intrinsic to the learner, and of which each is supposed to have a different fixed amount. Once it has been measured, what are teachers supposed to do about it? Only accept it, it seems, and limit the educational aspirations of pupils accordingly.

Criterion-Referenced Assessment: Describing Attainment

A much more positive view of what teachers and pupils can hope to achieve develops from thinking of "general ability" as simply *the collection of specific abilities (knowledge, skills, understanding) that a pupil has learned by a particular time*. These "abilities" are something teachers *can* work with, recognising, developing, consolidating and adding to them through classroom teaching and learning. If we think in this way, "ability" is no longer something intrinsic to the pupil, but something that changes continually, as the pupil learns new things and forgets others. Indeed the notion of "general ability" can be dropped altogether.

During the late 1970s researchers at Stirling University built up a body of evidence and argument in favour of this new view of ability (see McIntyre, 1978). To use this idea of ability, one must abandon the assumptions on which norm-referenced assessment is based. Global marks and relative grades are irrelevant: one needs *a description of what each pupil has learned, at a useful level of detail.* This was the conception of CRA developed at Stirling, but it was not the only one on offer. One problem facing the Scottish developments was that most of the work on criterion-referenced assessment had been done in America, often in the context of "minimal competency testing", designed to hold schools accountable for having all their students achieve certain standards in basic education. There, the emphasis was on a sophisticated technology of testing rooted in the behavioural objectives tradition and carried on by professional test constructors rather than teachers. Looking at the literature in this area (see Brown, 1981) compared with that on the design of traditional examinations, it is the similarity, not the difference, that is striking: the oppressive terminology, the emphasis on overall numerical scores, the obsessive search for statistical certainty about "standards" (that is, about the "correctness" of pass-marks and cut-off scores, but *not* about any attempt to state clearly what makes good or adequate answers different from those that are not).

It was not surprising that in these early days Scottish teachers developed a limited view of CRA centred on the notion of *tests* rather than a general approach to assessment. They had a variety of misapprehensions and misgivings. They foresaw excessive testing, using multiple choice items testing trivial behavioural outcomes: this was particularly worrying to teachers of the humanities. CRA appeared to be complicated and jargon-ridden (which appealed to some!). It seemed to be associated with the less able and with a high pass rate: was it not an attempt to conceal a watering down of standards? It might be appropriate in the teaching situation, but would we not still need NRA for prediction, guidance and selection, and above all for certification? Would the public not insist? Though the criterion-referencing lobby offered answers, these uncertainties grumbled away and surfaced repeatedly during the continuing debate that accompanied developments at every level.

In 1980 the Scottish Education Department (SED) set in motion a carefully coordinated programme of research related to the implementation of the Munn and Dunning reports (Scottish Education Department, 1977a and 1977b), now become the Standard Grade development programme for the Scottish Certificate of Education. Much of the research was concerned with assessment, and with CRA in particular. Projects covered most areas of the curriculum, and included work on diagnostic assessment, certification, item-banking, and a wide range of oral and practical skills (see Scottish Education Department, 1982a). Yet even as this work got under way, decisions were being taken which resulted in a further layer of confusion, and put the development of a truly criterion-referenced system of assessment in jeopardy.

The Emergence of GRC

In 1982 the provisional plan for the Standard Grade development was published as *A Framework for Decision* (Scottish Education Department, 1982b). One of the key concepts in the proposed certification system was that of Grade Related Criteria (GRC). These were described as

". . . broad indicators or descriptions of expected performance in key aspects of a given subject at different levels of award".

Working parties were already generating lists of GRC statements to describe several levels of performance in each of the various "elements" of their subjects.

GRC were presented as a mechanism to cope with some of the problems in the post-Dunning system of certification. This had initially envisaged three levels of award (Foundation, General and Credit) which might be associated with quite distinct syllabuses in at least some subjects. An obvious problem was that a pupil might embark on a course at a level which later proved unsuitable. However, if the GRC statements of performance could be made common to more than one syllabus then a misplaced candidate might still receive the "right" award at the end. The Standard Grade system also allowed school-based assessment to count directly towards certification, a new departure in Scotland at 16+. Here, GRC would be the key to moderation, the process by which the schools' standards of grading would be made to match those of the external examinations. Finally, GRC would be used in combining grades for different elements of the subject into an overall award.

In short, these statements were to provide the framework for the whole process of assessment for certification. It was hoped that they would also provide useful targets for teaching, and for formative assessment during the course.

Problems with GRC in Theory

But were GRC a form of criterion-referencing, and would they work? We argued that these two issues were closely linked, and that the answer to both questions was "No" (Drever, Munn, McIntyre and Mitchell, 1983).

Our main criticism was that the GRC-based framework and mechanisms depended on *treating as equivalent attainments which were clearly quite different.* Pupils on different courses must have been studying and learning different things: these should not be glibly equated. Internal assessment had been introduced specifically to test those attainments that external examinations could *not* reach. And why had working parties been at such pains to identify different elements of their subject, and develop "cognitive profiles" for reporting them separately, if these were then to be collapsed into an overall grade? All of this offended against our definition of criterion-referenced assessment, since you could not "describe what pupils had learned at a useful level of detail" if you insisted on blending everything together.

To accept the GRC approach one had to lapse into norm-referenced thinking, and accept the traditional view of assessment as a way of measuring "ability". In that case one could regard pupils' performance in the various elements as simply different manifestations of "general ability", so that in that sense they were all equivalent. So, if 50 per cent of pupils reached grade level 4 in the element Knowledge and Understanding, then we might suppose that 50 per cent would also reach grade level 4 in Problem-Solving, and write or adjust GRC statements to ensure that our "standards" were consistent across the elements. Of course in practice it might not be the same 50 per cent of pupils who attained these levels and an individual pupil might have a range of grades across elements. In a truly criterion-referenced system, this would be regarded as natural, and as providing "useful detail" about pupils' attainments. However, within the traditional framework, such variation is slightly embarrassing: a pupil's intrinsic "ability" really should not vary, so how can we get the true measure of it? Working parties debated this issue, in effect, as they tried to decide on rules for arriving at an overall grade. They usually decided on some form of averaging, and thus, in effect, they treated *significant detail* as mere *error of measurement*.

During this period of development, the insistence on an overall composite grade, the ready resort to numerical devices to combine different attainments, and some of the advice offered to working groups (for example that before thinking about grade descriptions they should "conjure up five pupils of your own who represent the top 10 per cent, next 20 per cent, middle 40 per cent and so on") helped to convince us that GRC would reinforce rather than challenge many features of existing thinking and practice, and especially the traditional view of "ability" as a fixed pupil characteristic, something to be measured rather than developed.

Nevertheless we recognised that GRC had a powerful appeal for decision makers whose perspective on assessment was administrative or political, rather than pedagogical. A system of grade-related criteria appeared to achieve two things at once, with commendable economy: it left the grading system untouched, thereby allowing easy selection by employers and colleges; and it met concern about accountability and "standards". It could claim that standards were being maintained, because it had now stated what a grade 3 award in Home Economics would *mean*, this year and every year.

Unfortunately these two goals came into conflict, because grading had been given priority over the setting of clear standards. Working parties were asked to generate descriptions of performance on a seven-point scale for each element. This begged the fundamental question of whether such a grading scale could actually represent the variation in performance. Did pupils' work fall easily into seven different types, each unambiguously "better" or "worse" than the others? It was at least conceivable that in some elements there might be only one or two distinct levels capable of clear description, while in others there might be simply a continuum of improvement. In yet other elements performances might not be "better" or "worse" but simply *different* from each other. After all, in our existing examinations, two pupils with the same mark had usually compiled it in quite different ways; a candidate with 60 might be weaker in some respects than one with 40; and the difference between a "B" and a "C" was in many cases less than the range within the "B"s. Indeed all our juggling with marks, weightings and statistics has been necessary because we have never yet put grading on any meaningful basis: the numbers game is a way of avoiding the difficulty of describing the complexity of what each candidate has learned. We foresaw that GRC might prove impossible to write with any clarity, and so, difficult to use with any precision. The difficulties might then be blamed on the introduction of CRA, when in fact that was only exposing a lack of validity in traditional grading.

Problems with GRC in Practice

Our misgivings were strengthened when the lists of GRC began to emerge. Because the overall framework was rigid, in order to force all the elements of every subject into it the GRC statements themselves had to be somewhat "flex-ible", or rather, vague and ambiguous. Sometimes the distinction between grades rested on how phrases such as "with some degree of success" or "for the most part" were interpreted, or on the distinction between "rudimentary" and "moderate" understanding. In other cases precision was achieved, but only by reverting to the numbers game: ". . . attainment of 80% of the Knowledge objectives for this Level".

Evidence accumulated that teachers were finding the GRC very difficult to apply. Unable to decide in which category to put a piece of work, they would resort to grading the *pupil*, in time honoured norm-referenced fashion. ("He's usually no more than a 5 . . . what does it say for 5? . . . well, I suppose that's probably about right.") An even more pressing problem was the sheer amount of work that the new schemes of assessment demanded of all teachers. Eventually "a substantial number of representa-tions were received by the Secretary of State [for Scotland] that assessment in Standard Grade courses was unduly complicated" (SGROAG Report, Scottish Education Department, 1986) and SGROAG (the Standard Grade Review of Assessment Group) was set up to suggest reforms. This body had available to it professional advice of various kinds, and also the findings of research projects connected with the development programme including one carried out by the Scottish Examination Board itself into the use of GRC in setting and marking examinations.

It was clear that grade levels were not sufficiently distinguishable. This was not surprising. We had seen GRC lumping together factors such as the amount learned, the difficulty of tasks, the adequacy of performance, and the amount of help given, in the desperate attempt to fit pupils' attainments into the ubiquitous seven-point scale. The result was that questions could not be matched to levels with any degree of reliability. Items designed to test, say, grade 5 ought to have been more difficult than those testing grade 6, but in practice an alarming degree of overlap was found. (Of course examiners have always found it difficult to predict or explain the difficulty of particular questions, but since this has been concealed within an overall score, our examinations have enjoyed a spurious reputation for fine-tuning.)

Similarly the elements did not show up as separate dimensions of performance within a subject. Scores for questions testing different elements often correlated just as well with one another as those intended to test the same element. One reaction to this was that we did not need separate elements at all, since they were all testing the same thing (presumably pupils' "ability"). This was to mistake the problem, which was that the elements had been devised as general *teaching* goals, and not as discrete categories of *attainment*. The curriculum developers in Standard Grade working parties had been concerned to shift the emphasis in the teaching of their subjects so as to promote the learning of general skills such as communication or problem-solving, and they had defined their elements accordingly. However, as SGROAG recognised, the elements as they stood were bundles of objectives, with only a general family resemblance in common. They did not necessarily reflect the structure of pupils' learning, nor the most helpful way of reporting it. (In particular, the evidence did not support the current enthusiasm for "content-free" skills. Rather it showed that learning and use of *content* and of *skills* were interdependent.)

The SGROAG Response: Keep it Simple

The GRC framework, intended to support Standard Grade assessment, was instead creating distortions and tensions that threatened the whole edifice. One could not realistically expect SGROAG to dismantle the framework. What they did suggest was simplification, with reduction in the number of elements and with only three grade levels to be fully defined by GRC. This on its own might seem like a retreat from precise description, and hence from criterion-referencing. However, it is better seen as a loosening of the straitjacket, allowing the possibility that clear description could be developed within particular areas such as the individual levels and elements within a subject, and that these in turn might be built together into a comprehensive criterion-referenced approach for that subject. Because the SGROAG report generally showed a tacit recognition and understanding of the problems arising from GRC there were grounds for renewed optimism about the eventual outcome.

SGROAG also reaffirmed the importance of assessment by teachers. Given the worsening industrial relations in schools it would have been understandable if they had opted simply to hand certification back to the external examiner, abandoning the new, interesting but difficult areas such as practical skills, oral discussion and experiential learning, in which assessment was mainly school-based. They did not do so. Instead they argued for a contribution to certification based on the whole body of evidence available in school through informal as well as formal assessment, and that teachers need not constrain assessment to fit the GRC until near the end of the course. One might see this as the traditional stance, that teachers can do as they like regarding assessment so long as at the finish they fit in with the external examination system. However, SGROAG's emphasis on assessment within teaching, and on the need for research on how GRC affect classroom practice, suggests a more positive interest in schools' internal assessment.

A school-based system of assessment for certification would have advantages, in principle, in relation to both validity and reliability. The main benefit, however, would be that there need no longer be a separation of "diagnostic" assessment to promote learning, and assessment for reporting and certification. One could grow out of the other, and teachers need not waste their efforts in helping pupils to beat the examiner. This in turn would make it easier to tackle a fundamental problem in devising a criterion-referenced system of assessment: that of ensuring that the details of pupils' day-to-day learning, which teachers assess in a criterion-referenced way, are clearly related to those attainments of longer-term learning goals that reports and certificates should make public. The norm-referenced tradition makes no attempt to do this, using the notion of "measuring ability" to justify various arbitrary numerical procedures by which detailed information is puréed into a meaningless grade.

Present curriculum plans, and the GRC framework, offer two main models of the relationship between short- and long-term attainment. In one we are given lists of precisely stated lesson outcomes, which do not "add up" in any obvious way to anything larger. For terminal assessment we simply count them to see if a passing score has been attained for, say, "Knowledge". In the other we are offered a broad description of some multi-faceted general skill to be assessed globally; teachers can then pick away as aspects and sub-aspects of it in their classroom work. Neither of these models provides a clear link between short- and long-term learning, and often teachers suppose that if they attend to the details, it is their pupils' "ability" which will decide whether or not they retain and synthesise the specific items of learning into "real" attainment.

The solution to the problem does not lie in new and equally arbitrary procedures for aggregating scores. It depends on identifying "abilities" on an intermediate scale, whose relationships to specific lesson activities and whose contributions to overall course goals can be clearly understood, and are not simply numerical artefacts.

Prospects for Further Development

In this brief account I have viewed Standard Grade from a particular perspective, as an attempt to move from norm-referenced measurement to criterion-referenced descriptions, and with an attendant struggle to possess and define the form of CRA. GRC must have seemed like a sensible compromise, but threatened to result in the worst of both worlds, retaining the pessimistic view of ability and the lack of meaning intrinsic to traditional grading, while being even more difficult to develop and operate than a properly criterion-referenced system. GRC represented a compromise of convenience from an administrative perspective, when what was needed was a conceptual synthesis from a perspective of teaching and learning.

The Dunning Report and the subsequent Standard Grade development have permanently changed the face of assessment in Scottish secondary schools. They have extended national certification in Scotland to the whole school population, and to all aspects of most subjects. School-based assessment is now accepted as part of certification, and the importance of assessment within teaching is fully recognised. In the course of this development many teachers have thought carefully and critically about the purposes of assessment and the nature and structure of the knowledge and skills that form the subject matter of their teaching. This new understanding offers a basis for further development in which each subject could continue to explore the ways in which pupils' learning builds up, and could experiment with different numbers of elements and levels, and different ways of reporting attainments: some as a profile, others as a series of stages reached, some as a list of tasks completed.

The ultimate aim would be to provide individualised descriptions of what pupils have learned, in simple prose, and based on what teachers think about and do in their classrooms, rather than on how they think and talk in the unreal hot-house context of working party discussions.

REFERENCES

Brown, S. (1980). *Introducing Criterion-referenced Assessment: Teachers' Views*, Stirling Educational Monographs, No. 7, Stirling: University of Stirling Department of Education.

Brown, S. (1981). *What Do They Know? A Review of Criterion-Referenced Assessment*, Edinburgh: HMSO.

Drever, E. (1987). *Mastery Learning in the Secondary School: a Report of School Based Research*, Stirling Educational Monographs, No. 17, Stirling: University of Stirling Department of Education.

Drever, E., Munn, P., McIntyre, D. and Mitchell, R. (1983). "'A Framework for Decision'—or—'Business as Usual'?", *Scottish Educational Review*, 15 (2), 83–91.

McIntyre, D. (1978). "Differences and differentiation among pupils", in McIntyre, D. (ed.), *A Critique of the Munn and Dunning Reports*, Stirling Educational Monographs, No. 4, Stirling: University of Stirling Department of Education.

Scottish Education Department (1977a). *Assessment for All (The Dunning Report)*, Edinburgh: HMSO.

Scottish Education Department (1977b). *The Structure of the Curriculum in the Third and Fourth Years of the Secondary School (The Munn Report)*, Edinburgh: HMSO.

Scottish Education Department (1982a). *The Munn and Dunning Reports: Interim Report on Research*, Edinburgh: SED (mimeo).

Scottish Education Department (1982b). *The Munn and Dunning Reports: Framework for Decision*, Edinburgh: SED (mimeo).

Scottish Education Department (1986). *Assessment in Standard Grade Courses: Proposals for Simplification (SGROAG Report)*, Edinburgh: SED (mimeo).

CHAPTER 7

THE NATIONAL CERTIFICATE

Harry Black
The Scottish Council for Research in Education

In Chapter 1 Sally Brown set out five themes for this book and indicated that each chapter would relate to at least some of them. This account of the Scottish "National Certificate", which is in essence an integrated programme of curricular modules and their associated assessment system validated by the Scottish Vocational Education Council (SCOTVEC), will embrace each, not because I feel obliged to conform to the structure of the book but because it is necessary to do so to reflect the aspirations of those who established the programme.

The Background

The roots of the National Certificate are to be found in a document published by the Scottish Education Department in 1983. *16–18s in Scotland: An Action Plan* (Scottish Education Department, 1983) asserted that the existing provision of externally validated certificates for non-advanced further education was confusing and cumbersome. In addition to the Scottish Business Education Council and the Scottish Technical Education Council, students in Scottish colleges could be following courses leading to the award of certificates by, for example, the City and Guilds of London Institute, the Royal Society of

Arts, and Pitmans. The nature of the certificates from these bodies varied and in some cases there was substantial overlap in provision in subject areas.

Perhaps equally important, since the mid 1970s there had been substantial development in thinking in Scotland about the nature and purpose of assessment. The Report of the "Dunning Committee" on assessment (Scottish Education Department, 1977a) and the associated report on the curriculum by the "Munn Committee" (Scottish Education Department, 1977b) had led to the establishment of the Scottish Certificate of Education Standard Grade courses for 14–16 year olds (see Chapter 6). It was felt necessary and appropriate, therefore, to ensure that the educational experiences of young people who had moved through Standard Grade courses should "articulate" with post-16 provision.

Development was rapid. Less than two years after the publication of the "Action Plan", the beginning of the academic session 1984/85 saw the launch of the new certificate. It was very different to what had preceded it and substantially different to Standard Grade. Courses of fixed term duration were replaced by modules each representing a notional 40 hour unit of study.

The scope was accommodated within nine broad categories including Interdisciplinary Studies, Business and Administration, Distribution Services, Engineering, Built Environment, Caring, Industrial Processing, Land and Sea Based Industries and Pure and Applied Sciences. For the first session 600 modules were available and at the time of writing the catalogue includes almost five times that number. Furthermore, the National Certificate has become the sole mode of accreditation for non-advanced further education in Scotland and has gained a substantial foothold in secondary schools especially in the fifth and sixth years, but also in the third and fourth, where it has come to complement (and, some might argue, threaten) Standard Grade.

What is in a Module Descriptor?

In Chapter 1 it was asserted that one feature of contemporary assessment development has been its close links with the curriculum. Not least because of this fundamental relationship, it is important before looking in detail at the assessment model itself to understand a little more about the nature of the National Certificate modules and indeed the whole curricular experience intended for young people studying them.

The intended nature of each module is laid out in a "module descriptor". Throughout the system each of these descriptors shares a set of common sub-divisions or sections although the scope and quality of these vary substantially.

The first section establishes the type and purpose of the module. General modules, as their name implies, have a range of possible applications. They might, for example, form the introductory part of a specialised course in something like baking or photography, or alternatively they could stand alone as part of a broader course or a curriculum designed to allow students to sample a range of experiences. Specialist modules will have less widespread application, and indeed in Scotland as a whole may be available in only a few centres. These will be the building blocks for a set of modules leading to acceptance as a vocational qualification in a wide range of forms of employment.

The second section sets out the preferred entry level for the module. Many, especially those of a general nature, do not require formal entry qualifications while others will indicate preference for a previous qualification at Standard Grade or attainment of another related module.

This is followed by the third section which is probably the most central and gives the first indication of the essential relationship between assessment and the curriculum. A number of learning outcomes are set out in loosely behavioural terms and it is mastery of these which will determine "success" or "failure". Thus, for example, in the *Travel and Tourism Study Visit* module, the learning outcomes are that the student should:

1. prepare a file of relevant pre-travel requirements and information for a visit outside Scotland;
2. know the attractions and amenities of a resort and their suitability for various client types;
3. know the range of accommodation available in a resort and its suitability for various client types;
4. know the functions of an employee directly involved in the travel industry within a resort.

The problem with brief behavioural statements such as these, of course, is that they are open to a wide range of interpretation. In relation to number one, for example, what is meant by "relevant", what length of visits would be appropriate and does "outside Scotland" include the rest of the world? Is he or she permitted to consult with colleagues (as would be the case in most travel shops)? The list of questions could go on much longer, but the essential message is that these statements in themselves leave much to personal interpretation; and in assessment terms that would lead one to ask questions about reliability.

The fourth section of the descriptor is designed to cope with this. This "Content/Context" list sets out appropriate foci for each of the learning outcomes. In relation to outcome 1 above, for example, it lists some of the materials and information which might be found in a "file of relevant information". But still there is no indication of whether Bristol, Benidorm and Brisbane, each of which is an appropriate focus "outside Scotland", would be equally acceptable. Is this a weakness in the approach, or does it reflect another feature of the assessment model being used?

There can be little doubt that in assessment terms the lack of clear "content limits" is likely to endanger the technical quality of assessments made. If lecturers in one college confine their teaching to, say, the popular

Mediterranean resorts, their students will have very different factual knowledge from those whose learning covers a much broader field, or focus on destinations favoured by business people rather than tourists. It would be difficult to judge whether learning in one context would be "easier" than in another, but the very fact that this is a question open to speculation suggests that neither teaching staff, SCOTVEC "quality control" personnel nor the end users in the travel trade can assume ease of comparison between students from different colleges.

But an alternative way of interpreting the situation is that this kind of thinking is addressing the wrong question. The important feature of the learning outcome is not knowing the "facts" about a large number of tourist spots but that the student should be able to prepare a file. This is a process-oriented objective and to an extent the content within which it is to be displayed is irrelevant. Its important characteristic is a transferable skill. And it is a particular feature of many of the contemporary assessment initiatives described in this book that processes and skills have replaced facts and knowledge recall as the kernel of the assessment system. The suggestion that at least in this particular module there is an unresolved ambiguity about content which could lead to quality control problems about reliability is a feature worthy of further attention, but the appropriate remedy would not simply be to spell out the content limits in terms of resorts.

The next section which is "Suggested Learning and Teaching Approaches" again emphasises the relationship envisaged amongst curriculum, teaching and assessment. For example, as will be discussed in greater detail below, central to the recommended strategies for many modules is an emphasis on student-centred learning and throughout the literature there is a commitment to the use of assessment for formative or diagnostic purposes as well as for certification. Teachers are encouraged to make clear to students what will be expected of them to master the learning outcomes and to use assessment to help students understand what they have achieved and where they should concentrate their efforts to overcome weaknesses.

The final common section of module descriptors also reflects a fundamental innovation in assessment, at least for this sector of education. "Assessment Procedures" indicates for each outcome what is considered to be an appropriate instrument of assessment and the performance criteria which establish the kind of evidence the student must produce in order to achieve mastery. This section is necessary because, with a very few exceptions, award of the module is college-based and indeed typically does not depend on an "end of module" test, but instead, on assessment carried on throughout the teaching and learning process.

The Assessment Model

Module descriptors are obviously important in establishing the nature and focus of the learning experience. But for assessment purposes they can also be thought of as the resource which teachers use to apply the overall National Certificate assessment model in a particular context. To an extent, having looked at the features of descriptors has established the agenda for describing the model. But what are its essential features?

First, it is clear that it does not purport to comment on "general ability" in a subject or area of study. In fact, it is difficult to associate the notion of "ability" with this model. Instead it sets out to describe students' attainments of clearly set out goals which are known to both student and teacher in advance. These attainments may well constitute a good set of skills with which to tackle some specific vocational task but the appropriate message to be read from the certificate is that the student "has done" x, y and z.

Now this is a somewhat different conceptualisation of attainment to that associated with most "measures" of general ability in a subject. An "A-level" French for example, at least in popular opinion, conveys a message about what a student "can do". But how many A-level French "can do's" can remember what the past historic looks like, never mind write in it? Certainly for me much of my schooltime attainments in mathematics and science, for example, should be construed as "used to be able to's" rather than "can do's", and I would suggest that this is the case for much of what is the established currency of qualifications.

The second important feature of the model is that students are assessed against what are considered to be clearly defined performance criteria rather than comparing their performance with that of their peers. This, combined with the focus on clearly set out goals noted above, places the assessment model firmly in the "criterion-referenced" category.

It should be recognised that "criterion-referenced assessment" is a general model which embraces substantial diversity both in variety and in quality. Thus the National Certificate is an application based on dichotomous distinctions between "mastery" and "non-mastery". Students either have or have not mastered a learning outcome and there is no implication of greater or lesser competence in relation to a broader domain. In contrast, Standard Grade is essentially a multiple cut-score application which has set out to establish a graded scale of attainment in relation, for example, to "speaking" in English or "investigating" in the social subjects. There is no space in this paper to compare and contrast these alternative applications of criterion-referenced assessment but it might be appropriate to reflect on the relative complexity of assessing mastery of "investigating" in general compared with, for example, one of the intended outcomes listed in the Travel and Tourism module described above. If the domain to be assessed is large in scale and embraces the use of a skill in many different circumstances, it is not at all easy to design a brief test to sample attainment nor is it possible to arrive at a defensible decision based on the observation of only a limited number of opportunities to display mastery in a practical setting. In contrast, if the domain is tightly defined and limited in scope, the chances of reliable assessment are substantially increased. In short, the National Certificate, which at least in theory allows assessment to focus on a number of small-scale domains would appear to be an application which could yield reliable assessments.

The third important feature of the model is that decisions on student attainment are school or college based. There is also substantial emphasis on assessment arising naturally out of the learning context rather than being dependent on formal testing at specific points such as the end of the module. Of course whether this "naturalistic" assessment in fact takes place or whether staff in the confines of their own teaching environments rely on more traditional approaches is difficult to determine. What is the case, however, is that a system which until the mid-1980s relied almost entirely on external examinations for certificate purposes has been replaced by a school or college based model with "moderation" by SCOTVEC and at least superficially the change has worked.

The fourth feature of the model which seems to be important is that the original "Action Plan", subsequent official documents and many of the module descriptors themselves emphasise the importance of assessment in the broad sense and not just as an adjunct to certification.

To an extent this follows from the choice of criterion-referenced assessment as the basic model. Its roots lie in the inadequacy of norm-referenced assessment to provide adequate descriptions of success or lack of it. Thus in the 1960s when programmed learning was an approach of considerable interest, a number of educationists were frustrated by the lack of a sound assessment model which would describe what a student had or had not understood as opposed to measuring the extent to which one student appeared to know more about a topic than another (Glaser, 1963; Popham, 1969 and 1971). The paradigms for item choice, which relied on correlational discrimination techniques, and the notions of success and failure, which related more to other students than to the topic under consideration, were questioned and a new technology for assessment emerged. The origins of criterion-referenced assessment in a pedagogic problem thus contrast substantially with norm-referenced assessment. The origins of norm-referencing lie in the psychometric problems of sorting amongst servicemen in World War I for some notion of "intelligence". But the influence of intelligence testing by psychologists extended rapidly into education and was manifested, for example, by the 11+ examination in Britain and in much of the testing which is still carried out in the United States today.

Put simply, therefore, while the concerns of norm-referenced assessment are about sorting and choosing, the concerns of criterion-referenced assessment are about description and pedagogic utility. And while it is difficult to show empirically, one suspects that it is the latter feature which has convinced decision-makers that a shift in the model for certification is desirable. An assessment model which can clearly set out goals for teacher and student and identify the strengths and weaknesses of individual students, curricula and teaching strategies, is potentially a powerful tool for the classroom. It also appeals to notions of equity because success does not depend on the achievements of one's peers but on one's own efforts and the democratic nature of the environment (because the criteria for success are open to inspection by all interested parties). One suspects that the substantial emphasis placed in official documents on the broader purposes of assessment and on the potential for student-centred learning reflects the persuasive nature of these features of the model; what remains to be seen, of course, is the extent to which policy and theory have been turned into practice in the school, the college and the workplace.

The final feature of the model which is worthy of particular note lies more clearly in its role as a summative certificate which can be used as a key to further studies but also, and perhaps more typically, as a qualification with which to seek employment. This feature is its potential to deliver a profile of attainment both within individual modules and across the series studied by students. This is particularly interesting because the way in which criterion-referenced assessment has been interpreted over the whole range of modules is substantially broader than the narrow foci of much of the programmed learning materials where it had its origins.

Within any given module, attainment is recorded on the certificate as wholly complete, or if only some of the outcomes have been mastered, these are recorded and the module is shown as only partially completed. Students have the option at some later stage to finish partially completed modules if they can provide evidence of having mastered the as yet uncompleted learning outcomes.

This leaves open the possibility for potential users of modules to ascertain what exactly students who have mastered a given module have learned. If they know, for example, that in order to carry out a certain task without further training a prospective employee must have certain skills, they can specify the modules required. Furthermore, employers have the opportunity to decide in advance the profile of competencies they require for particular tasks, and day-release training can be tailored around these needs through a student following an agreed programme of modules.

Quite whether such sophisticated use of the system materialises as common practice depends on two variables. First, employers will have to clarify their thinking on the skills and competencies required of prospective employees (or those on staff who are involved in training) to be able to identify what in fact they do need to know or be able to do. It is not at all clear whether this has yet been achieved. But second, and perhaps more important for educationists, the quality control mechanism both within colleges and at a national level must develop to the point where users of such modules can rely on the messages about student attainment conveyed by them.

In summary, therefore, the National Certificate is a record of modules and their learning outcomes which have been achieved by a student. Decisions on the mastery of these outcomes is by college (or school or workplace) based criterion-referenced assessment and the quality of these assessments is the responsibility of SCOTVEC and its moderation system.

The National Certificate in Practice

Up to this point the paper has set out to provide a descriptive critique of the nature of the National Certificate and the assessment model on which it is based. But to what extent does practice on the ground reflect this theory and aspiration? This is a difficult question to respond to, not least because the system is such a recent innovation, but a first report from a research project by the Scottish Council for Research in Education may give some clues about the answer and about some of the more specific questions it may be appropriate to ask. It is important to note, however, that the findings were based on interviews with staff and questionnaires to students in only fourteen departments and cannot be considered to be "generalisable" in any way other than that appropriate to a case study design. The "Assessment in the National Certificate" Project, 1985–88, was funded by the Scottish Education Department. (The first report of the Project which considers the perceptions of the approach held by staff in 14 case study departments will shortly be available and further reports are expected at a later date.)

The evidence indicated that in these case study departments, the clarification of goals through the use of module descriptors did not pose many problems for staff and, indeed, was welcomed by some as a useful guide to their teaching. For a few, and especially those involved with communications modules, there was a fear that the approach could be inflexible. Overall, however, there was a general acceptance of the model and there were few instances of staff bemoaning the demise of the external examination and the syllabus which had gone with it.

The reaction to criterion-referenced assessment in itself was more mixed. Almost all staff recognised that it had substantial potential to motivate slower attainers, but doubt was expressed by some about its impact on rapid attainers. In fact, the comments used related not to slow and rapid attainers, but to more or less "able" students which is an interesting reflection on the all-pervasive influence of the concept even in a context where specific attainments are intended to be the currency of comparison rather than general ability.

But what was perhaps least encouraging was that the staff in most of the case studies looked at were not capitalising on the potential of the model to provide formative or diagnostic information for their students. For some it seemed likely that little real thought had been given to this. For others there were perceived problems in managing assessment within the 40 hour block committed to modules, and this was especially true in those case studies where the descriptions of teaching indicated a rather mechanistic approach with each intended outcome and its associated assessment taking place in a rigid lock-step pattern. In the case study departments where groups of modules were taught together in a larger block of time, there seemed to be greater scope for differentiation and consequently greater use of assessment for formative or diagnostic purposes as well as to fulfil the summative requirements.

These findings were particularly interesting to compare with the views of the students. It was clear that the students aspired to using the assessment process as a formative resource and put substantial value on its indicating to them the areas in which they were having difficulty. Nor was this the first time that in SCRE's assessment work it had been established that while the emphasis amongst teachers was on the summative purpose, the hope of students (and their parents) was that it would also be used for diagnostic or formative reasons (Dockrell and McKay, 1983; Black and Dockrell, 1984). It would seem that expressing commitment to the broader purposes of assessment in policy terms is easier to achieve than it is to put it into practice, but the fact that some teachers manage to implement it and a large proportion of students would welcome it suggests that it is a feature of the relationship amongst teaching and assessment in National Certificate learning situations which would deserve of greater attention.

The findings on the more technical features of National Certificate assessment in this project should also be understood clearly to reflect what the case study staff perceived to be the case rather than the product of detailed empirical analysis of the assessments themselves.

Although the staff interviewed did not have (nor did they claim to have) a sophisticated technical understanding of issues such as validity, reliability and generalisability, it appeared that most were reasonably confident that the assessments they themselves were making were valid and reliable at least in the sense of their being consistent. However, the extent to which they felt confident about inter-rater reliability even within, but more emphatically between, colleges varied substantially. There was not a great confidence that the SCOTVEC "quality control" system was adequate on its own for this purpose at least in part because the resources available were inadequate for the task. One college in particular was part of a substantial programme of regional moderation which was designed to support assessment and maintain local standards. But perhaps most important in this regard, the resource which staff valued most in helping them implement and maintain their own assessment strategy was the help of their colleagues. There was circumstantial evidence that implementing the National Certificate, at least in some of the colleges looked at, had encouraged the development not only of closer links between colleagues in the same department but also between departments and this had proved a substantial benefit to those involved.

There were, however, technical difficulties which had not been resolved by such support. In some cases the researchers felt that ambiguity and lack of clarity in the module descriptors was creating difficulties. Where "cut-scores" were not tied to a clear behavioural statement, or appealed to the exercise of professional judgement, it seemed likely that unreliability might creep in. In two case studies at least, staff seemed to be varying the performance criteria required according to what they felt to be the needs of particular groups of students such as YTS trainees, or traditional craft groups. This may or may not be appropriate for pedagogic purposes but it is surely questionable practice if the assumption end-users are asked to make is that anyone holding the same certificate has mastered the given learning outcomes in the way they are set out in the module descriptors.

Overview

This paper began by asserting that it would relate to all five of the basic themes for the book. In what way has this proven to be the case?

First, it must be clear that although the topic was a system of nationally accredited certification, it was impossible to describe the National Certificate without considering the broad purposes of assessment and its symbiotic relationship with teaching and the curriculum. This was because these relationships were established within the fundamental design of the system and not left to chance. It is on the extent to which these relationships develop and provide a stimulating and flexible teaching and learning environment that the initiative will be judged, and not just whether it will provide valid and reliable assessments although, as has been argued, this cannot be ignored.

Equally, it will be clear that the nature of attainment and the range of foci represented are radically different from the "general attainment" messages conveyed by traditional systems of external certification. Much of what is important in the National Certificate comprises the application of concepts and skills rather than the recall of facts. Furthermore, the importance of these outcomes is reflected in the kinds of assessment recommended and the contexts in which it is expected to take place. Since it is what is assessed which so often determines what will be valued by student and teacher in their learning and their teaching, it would seem reasonable to speculate that this will produce net benefits for the educational process if in nothing other than relevance.

The third major characteristic hypothesised for contemporary assessment developments was that they would be centred on a criterion-referenced model. It is probably important to recognise that the essential change is towards a criterion-referenced "frame" of assessment design as opposed to a norm-referenced frame. That is to say that the starting point for assessment is a description of "an individual's status with respect to a well-defined behaviour domain" (Popham, 1975) rather than a model to discriminate amongst individuals in relation to their respective performance on an appropriately constructed instrument. But the way in which this "frame" is manifested varies substantially and it could be contentious to claim that one interpretation is "better" than another.

At least in theory, however, the National Certificate approach to criterion-referenced assessment is probably closer to established practice in the field than most other applications in the United Kingdom. If there is a particular weakness it is probably that the content limits of some modules leave substantial scope for different interpretations of the domain to be assessed, and for some intended outcomes the performance criteria rely substantially on "professional judgement" which may or may not lead to reliable assessments. Whether these are inevitable features of an attempt to apply the criterion-referenced frame to such diverse domains, or are simply teething troubles in the early development of the SCOTVEC model, remains to be seen.

The system very clearly exemplifies an approach to certification where the responsibility for assessment has been devolved. Not only is assessment the responsibility of the teacher, but it is expected to take place in a variety of contexts and at times which are mutually advantageous to the teacher and the student. As was suggested in Chapter 2, it would appear to have wide potential in the workplace and can be used within systems of open learning and to generate profiles of attainment rather than reports on the basis of overall attainment.

Acknowledgement

The author wishes to acknowledge the support of John Hall, Sue Martin and John Yates of the SCRE "Assessment in the National Certificate" Project team in developing most of the ideas in this paper.

REFERENCES

Black, H. D. and Dockrell, W. B. (1984). *Criterion-Referenced Assessment in the Classroom*, Edinburgh, SCRE.

CHAPTER 8

SO WHAT HAS CHANGED?

Sally Brown
Scottish Council for Research in Education

The various contributors to this book have approached the
changing face of assessment from different perspectives.
In so doing they have demonstrated several important
features: the need to use both research findings and
practical experience to develop a full understanding of
assessment; the similarities and differences between assessment within and outwith educational institutions; how
much can be learned both from fundamental critiques of
certification systems and from approaches which take the
system for granted and then look at the problems and
possibilities which arise from its implementation; and how
the form which the assessment takes determines whether
teaching and learning is controlled by the state, the
educational institutions, the teachers or the young people
themselves.

Despite their different perspectives there are common
strands among the contributors. Some of those strands
were identified in the five themes of Chapter 1: the broader
concept of assessment, in terms of its purposes and closer
integration with teaching and learning; the increasing
range of young people's achievements and qualities
towards which assessment is directed in both traditional
and new contexts; the move towards assessment which
emphasises description rather than comparative judgements; the changes in ideas about who should have

responsibility for making the assessments; and the emerging recognition that formal certification should not be restricted to the privileged few.

The rest of this chapter provides a brief account of some of the light which has been shed on these themes by the contributions from Mary Simpson on diagnostic assessment, Lindsay Mitchell on assessment in the Youth Training Scheme (YTS), Julie Bowen on self-assessment in the Technical and Vocational Education Initiative (TVEI), Sally Brown and Harry Black on Records of Achievement (ROAs) and profiles, Eric Drever on criterion-referencing and Grade Related Criteria (GRC) in the Scottish Standard Grade and Harry Black on modular criterion-referenced assessment in the Scottish National Certificate.

A Broader Concept of Assessment

There is still evidence that much effort is put into using assessment as a tool for sorting out young people. We have moved on, however, to a widespread acceptance that assessment also has other purposes, which many see as more important than selection, and that selection itself has to be carried out in more detailed and insightful ways than the blunt grading methods of the past.

Certification in the compulsory and post-compulsory periods of education, the traditional tool for selection, is one of the areas where new developments are evident. The relationship which certification has had in the past with psychological testing of a norm-referenced kind is cracking and the new models, introduced in the Scottish Certificate of Education Standard Grade and the National Certificate, have moved towards descriptive or criterion-referenced systems. Such systems are seen as providing a support for teaching and learning through the opportunities they offer to introduce diagnostic assessment, motivate young people and evaluate curricula and teaching. In both these examples of certification the assessment and the curriculum are seen as strongly related.

There, however, the similarities between the two end. In the case of Standard Grade, the developments have attempted the ambitious task of constructing a system which by the introduction of GRC attempts to retain the apparent simplicity of the single grades awarded in the past, and at the same time to provide detailed descriptions of achievements to inform teaching and learning. It is clear that the price to be paid for trying to be all things to all people, whether of a norm- or criterion-referenced turn of mind, is a very complex system which has to make major, and questionable, assumptions about the structure of knowledge and pupils' learning. The National Certificate, in contrast, has abandoned the notion of single grades and of overall discrimination among students. It provides for each student on each module of work a description, of a dichotomous mastery/non-mastery kind, of his or her achievements in relation to each specified learning outcome. The account it gives of what has been achieved is much less vague than that for Standard Grade, but it does not offer any indication of how some students may have mastered some modules better than others, or better than other students.

Whether in practice these multiple purposes for the assessments are all fulfilled is a moot point. Although the rhetoric of both of these certification systems encourages the use of assessment to promote learning, it seems that in practice the potential of diagnostic and formative assessment in the modular work of the National Certificate is not being exploited. And in Standard Grade the covert concern with young people's general ability, which is a feature of GRC, undermines the other functions of assessment where the focus is on information about specific achievements in particular areas. The arguments for introducing ROAs or profiles directly address this issue of the mutual reinforcement of, on the one hand, the diagnostic or formative *processes* of assessment and, on the other hand, the *product* of assessment to provide a report or certificate. ROAs are seen as particularly flexible, multi-purpose, providing opportunities for records or reports on a much broader base than in the past, offering teachers more detailed information about their students, avoiding the distortion of accounts of achievements in different areas of knowledge (which follows when all are constrained within a single form of reporting), promoting self-aware-ness in young people themselves and encouraging closer relationships and dialogue between teacher and student.

The extent to which ROAs and profiling will reap the advantages they promise remains to be seen. The limited experiments on their introduction show how vulnerable is their effective implementation to the attitudes and influence of those who see them as loose, of low esteem and a threat to traditional standards in education.

A practical example of the implementation of profiling is offered by the Fife TVEI development. This scheme aims to make use of student self-assessment to encourage and inform both teaching and learning. The assessment is specifically designed to motivate students to assist them to reflect on their own experiences and to help them to consolidate their learning. Because the assessment, the students' learning and the decisions about the teaching are so closely interwoven in this development, the teachers also use students' self-assessments as a factor in their evaluation of their innovative programme.

It is in the area of diagnostic assessment, however, that the necessity of treating assessment as an integral part of the teaching and learning process is most extensively and persuasively articulated. The examination-oriented traditional system concentrated on identifying who was "best" and "worst" and who would do badly or well in the future; whatever its merits, that system also led to young people's demotivation and disaffection, it had poor predic-tive power, it failed to show teachers how pupils' learning could be improved and it did not provide employers with reliable and useful accounts of what their prospective employees could do. Where the priority is for assessment as a diagnostic process the aim is to understand the causes of difficulties and successes in learning, to prevent rather than cure problems in that learning and, thereby, to promote improvements in performance; that is to serve pupils rather than to sort them.

Teachers who might wish to implement such an approach face various difficulties. They have virtually no guidance on genuine diagnostic procedures from official documents; such documents offer little practical advice and frequently assume diagnosis to be simply a process of mapping out pupils' areas of failure, rather than of identifying the underlying causes of that failure. If the causes of failure remain unknown, however, the chance of effective remediation is slight, and this is reflected in the very modest achievements of the fairly primitive approaches to remediation (e.g. repetition of assessment and remedial loops) extant in classrooms. Diagnosis, it is argued, requires the teacher rather than the pupil to find answers, and the questions to be addressed are searching: "What has the pupil actually learned, right or wrong, from my teaching?", "Why did what was learned make more sense to the pupil than what I intended?", "What was it in the pupil's experience which caused erroneous learning?" and "What was it in what was taught which caused him or her to misunderstand?".

This approach to diagnostic assessment is based on a large body of international research which demonstrates that what is learned by a young person is profoundly influenced by what he or she already knows; much of that existing knowledge may be misconceived and act as a barrier to new learning. Such misconceptions may be manifest in assessment exercises, and they are most likely to be displayed in wrong rather than correct answers. It should be possible, therefore, to build into test items the identification of pupils' misconceptions. Unfortunately, existing items do this only rarely.

All of the cases cited above which express concern for assessment to widen its purposes beyond selection are contained within the debate about what goes on in schools and colleges, and in relation to institutionalised curricula. In other circumstances, however, such as the YTS, assessment's intended function is to help create a more adaptable and versatile workforce within a system which is constantly open to change. The context of the assessment is the workplace, and the concern is not so much with selection as with accreditation and a realistic judgement of whether a young person is able to perform the tasks required of him or her in that workplace. But because assessment forms an integral part of the training for employment, diagnostic or formative purposes are emphasised alongside accreditation. One particular problem to be faced in this field is brought about by the specific requirements for training in any given workplace: assessment designed to best suit the competences required by an individual company may not be the assessment best suited for general (national) accreditation across an industry or industries, and for preparing a flexible workforce which is open and ready for change.

It is already clear, therefore, that with assessment directed towards an increasing variety of functions, the focus is likely to be on a much broader range of young people's achievements and qualities. What do the contributions to this book tell us about that range?

A Wider Focus and New Contexts for Assessment

Formal certificates are expanding. The Standard Grade awards will be available in areas not previously covered by its predecessor the Ordinary Grade; it will include such things as physical education and multidisciplinary courses, and "science" will complement the traditional physics, chemistry and biology. Furthermore, competences not previously considered for certification, such as talking and listening in English or practical skills and handling information in science, are now assessed and reported. And at the post-compulsory stage a range of nine areas, with a strong vocational flavour, are the focus of National Certificate modules. Within this scheme a new emphasis is placed on achievements relating to the application of concepts and on skills, rather than recall of knowledge.

If ROAs and profiles are introduced on a wide scale, they will offer the possibility of including such things as young people's attitudes, problem-solving capabilities, competence in social interaction, personal qualities, creativity and other attributes which have not been amenable to assessment by formal test or examination. One example of this, the student self-assessments of the Fife TVEI scheme, is concerned with attributes very different from, and more extensive than, those with which we are familiar on traditional certificates. They relate to students' interests, abilities, relationships, skills and experiences, and may include assessment of characteristics like confidence, imagination and perseverence; aspects of academic achievement which are covered by formal measures in public examinations are not normally included. This profile endeavours to cover a range of personal and social skills as well as core skills (which are common to many tasks), and the assessments are made in all the relevant contexts: the classroom, work experience placements, on visits and in community work.

It is, however, the arguments for diagnostic assessment in schools and colleges which illustrate most vividly the breadth of concerns encompassed by the totality of assessment. Effective learning of all kinds depends on the schemata which are established in the long-term memory store of the young person. It may be necessary, therefore, at some time to access through diagnostic processes any or all of that information if teaching and curricula are to be designed appropriately to promote learning. In theory then, everything is up for the assessment grab.

A very large proportion of assessment is carried out in school or in college and so is concerned with getting young people to accomplish something in a simulated environment. Often those simulations are a poor reflection of the real thing: we ask students to behave as if they were scientists, or mathematicians, or historians, or travel writers under test conditions which have none of the opportunities for consulting references, contacts and conversations with other people, extended time or other features which characterise those kinds of activities in real life. Assessment in the YTS scheme, however, is concerned with real behaviour in real workplaces; with all the competences displayed in work and not just the sample that would be available during a curtailed test; with the young person's whole role rather than isolated skills in discrete elements; with the application of skills and knowledge in purposeful activity rather than in the abstract; with judgements of competence against actual standards used in the work context and not simply hypothesised as appropriate; and with all the effects that the conditions, pressures and demands of the workplace exert on real occupational competence.

Assessment of these kinds of skills and knowledge presents substantial problems for YTS. The aim is to concentrate on competences which are transferable from company to company, or industry to industry, rather than on those specific to one workplace. But the assumptions which are made about the generalisability of competences across contexts, and the abilities to transfer such competences from one workplace to another, have still to be tested. Political enthusiasm for the notion of education for generalised and transferable skills has outstripped our basic knowledge of whether such skills exist and, if so, how to assess them and their transfer. In a similar way, the development of young people's "personal effectiveness" at work is unanimously called for; but desirable though it may be, what it means and how it might be assessed are still pretty much of a mystery.

The extension of the range of qualities to be assessed in all these different educational or training contexts would have little meaning if information about the different elements was collapsed into a single grade or mark. Consideration of how more descriptive approaches might be used to formulate and communicate accounts of achievement is of substantial importance.

Assessment as Description

"A form of assessment which describes what has been achieved at a useful level of detail" is a helpful working definition of criterion-referenced assessment. Developments in Standard Grade endeavoured to achieve something of this sort, but at the same time went to considerable lengths to retain overall grades through GRC. This course of action inevitably encountered difficulties. On the one hand, there was a desire to identify the specific achievements which characterise any given area of the curriculum, and to report on individuals' performances on those distinctive aspects. Such an approach eschews the idea that performance on all aspects is determined by some underlying "general ability" in the subject, and accepts that young people may perform at different levels on different aspects. On the other hand, implicit in the notion of a single grade of overall performance across all aspects there is an assumption of some general ability which can be ascertained by some kind of aggregation or averaging across aspects, and for which individual's non-uniformity of performance on different aspects will be a nuisance and embarrassment.

This attempt to achieve description *and* grading (criterion-referencing and norm-referencing) at a stroke, has resulted in some rather dubious assumptions being made and the generation of a complicated system of assessment. It seems unlikely, for example, that the assumption that all kinds of pupil performance, no matter the nature of the knowledge and skills involved, can be adequately described by a fixed number of levels (formerly seven, now three) is a valid one. And it is not surprising that to identify and distinguish between these levels it has been necessary to include in the criterion statements complex combinations of the amount learned, task difficulty and extent of help given.

The national certificate has clearly abandoned the overall grade. In so doing it has relinquished the possibility of making simple comparisons among young people, and the concept of "general ability" as the crucial factor is dropped. Its descriptions of achievement relate directly to an integral part of the modular curriculum: the learning outcomes for each module. Its interpretation of the "useful detail" from criterion-referencing is a statement that the young person has, or has not, mastered a particular module or learning outcome. This is elaborated by the module specification which includes an account of the behaviours required, the content and the contexts in which those behaviours will be learned and displayed. Every effort is made, therefore, to ensure that not only teachers and certificate users but also the young people themselves are clear about what the goals are.

This may seem a neater and more precise approach than the descriptions of Standard Grade, but it has its drawbacks. It does not serve well those areas of the curriculum which are not amenable to precise statements of behavioural outcomes (for example, Caring or Personal and Social Development modules). Even where behavioural outcomes are readily identified, there will be differences between good and less good performances and a mastery/non-mastery scheme cannot take account of such differences. And in those modules where it appears that performance criteria can be objectively identified, teachers seem to set different standards according to their own views of what different groups (e.g. YTS or craft groups) are capable of achieving.

A central justification for the introduction of profiles or ROAs has referred to the opportunity it offers for complete descriptions of the achievements and experiences of young people in education and training. Where students are assessing themselves, using profiles, it has been suggested that the aim is to generate a description of the whole person including personal qualities, experiences and progress. Descriptive profiles, therefore, can cope with conflicting assessments made by different people, rather than trying to "iron them out", and such conflict may well indicate particularly interesting differences in perspectives; these differences would be camouflaged by the "averaging out" procedure which would be necessary if the aim were to provide a single overall grade. The profile is sufficiently flexible, furthermore, to allow descriptive information to be displayed alongside such measures as "O" grade results, and to permit assessments made by teachers, students, employers and examination boards to appear on the same document.

As well as in the school, ROAs have a place in work-based assessment. The criterion-referenced profile for YTS, compiled to standards required by employers, was designed to provide a useful description of achievement in that vocational programme. The whole basis of the approach requires the descriptive form since an overall judgement (mark, grade, rank order) would offer no information on the capability or readines to undertake a particular kind of work. Furthermore, a description can extend to include an account of the conditions under which the competence was being displayed.

All of this discussion has been directed towards the justification of descriptive reports or records of achievement. The developments in this direction, however, have enabled claims to be made that the assessments can fulfil other functions as well as reporting and recording. It goes without saying that assessment which provides descriptions of achievements is a necessary (but not sufficient) requirement for diagnostic assessment. Global grades or marks provide no guidance for action. It has further been argued that as part of diagnosis teachers have to extend their concern from a superficial assessment of what young people get right in tests to the many frameworks of knowledge which they build up in their minds from their experiences both within and outwith school. In particular, it is important to identify what someone starting a new course needs to know or be able to do and, through assessment and appropriately directed remediation, make sure that they acquire the necessary pre-requisite knowledge.

It is clear that the kinds of qualities which are the focus of assessment for its different purposes, and the variety of descriptive accounts which are called for, imply that responsibility for making the assessments will lie in several different quarters. Some of those have been identified by the contributors to this book.

Shifting the Responsibility for Assessment

Where there is concern that assessment should fulfil purposes like diagnosis of pupils' learning it is clear that much responsibility will fall on the teacher. The importance of teachers knowing about the misconceptions and understandings which pupils have has been stressed, but there is evidence of errors in many teachers' existing assumptions about their pupils' difficulties. It has been suggested that more realistic appraisal could be achieved if teachers were aware of how crucial it is to listen intently and extensively to what pupils *say*. This may well be a much more effective (in the sense of promoting learning) approach to assessment than all the formal or written end of topic and objectives-related tests which punctuate a school career.

There can be little argument about the centrality of the teachers' role in diagnostic assessment. Reservations about their capabilities to assess for certification purposes have been more frequently, and often unjustifiably, expressed. In both Standard Grade and the National Certificate, however, it has been accepted that the teacher or lecturer is well placed to assess those aspects of achievement which examinations (particularly the external variety) cannot reach.

For Standard Grade only some of the assessment is the responsibility of the school; the rest remains with the Scottish Examination Board. The partial devolution, however, marks some recognition that the inclusion of elements of school-based assessment is capable of providing a more complete, valid and reliable account than a purely external examination. It may also have spin-offs within the school manifest as the closer integration of diagnostic assessment and assessment for reporting purposes, an appreciation among teachers of the importance of assessment as part of teaching, a readiness on their part to reflect on the purposes of assessment, and an opportunity for them to consider the nature of the knowledge and skills which make up the subject matter of their teaching. In practice, the involvement of teachers in the assessment has led them to initiate public debate on the validity of, and demands made by, the GRC. The response to this from the Scottish Education Department's Standard Grade Review of Assessment Group, provided a rather better and simplified model for the assessment and a call for research on how GRC influence classroom practice.

The National Certificate module assessment is entirely school or college based with external moderation. It has emphasised the point that assessment should take place as and when it is most advantageous to student progress. There is no terminal examination, and the form and frequency of assessment varies from module to module and college to college. Considerable questions still have to be asked about the quality and reliability of the assessment across the country, and moderation procedures are at a relatively primitive stage. Nevertheless, evidence of the improving professionalism of lecturers in the development and integration of assessment into their teaching is starting to emerge.

In a context such as YTS we have circumstances where employers, or supervisors in the workplace, have to have the major role in assessment and the preparation of ROAs. The obvious justification for this is that they are best placed to make the judgements and, although they may have had little formal experience, many have been involved in informal assessment in the past. There are, however, some problems. "Supervisors" are sometimes quite junior and inexperienced themselves, and many will require training which is costly in time and money. Such staff development, of course, may well pay off in improved competence across the board, and it will certainly be necessary if valid, reliable and useful assessments are to be established in the environment of work.

Perhaps the most radical devolution of responsibility for assessment is that which gives it to the young people themselves. The Fife TVEI development provides one of the most ambitious schemes of this kind in the United Kingdom. The scheme is justified in terms of the support it provides for students' learning, the improvement in communication between teacher and student, the increase in validity for assessment in some (personal) areas, the raising of students' self-awareness and the way it better reflects the processes of assessment in "real life". Because such a high value is put on the process, self-assessment is included in both formative and summative aspects of the assessment scheme. The suitability of its use for summative purposes, however, is the subject of some debate in the literature.

Some arguments for self-assessment profiles look forward to democratic teacher-student negotiation to decide what will be assessed, and so to relinquish some of the teachers' control of the curriculum. In the Fife TVEI scheme, democracy does not go so far, but there is substantial teacher-student dialogue about the assessments themselves. There is, therefore, no real negotiation on the curriculum and targets for assessment, but there has been a substantial move from assessment which is "done to" students, towards that which is "done by" students.

There is no question that assessment is regarded now as a crucial element in the education of all young people. But it could be argued that this has always been the case and that what is new is the notion that there should be *certification* for everyone.

Certification for All

The notion of what counts as a certificate has moved on substantially over the last few years from the documents which lent themselves to being framed and hung up on walls for all to see. Nowadays certificates are available, in some form, to almost all young people who undertake education or training; they may run to several pages and require much more than a cursory glance if the meaning of the information they provide is to be understood and appropriately used.

There is still a firm emphasis on those forms of certification which have national currency, but local certificates are increasingly seen as of value and probably of higher validity than those which make claim to comparability across the country. The Fife TVEI scheme summary profile provides an example of a local certificate available to all the young people involved in the initiative. To what extent it and others like it will be useful and credible, and will be seen as valuable by students who are seeking employment or further education, remains to be seen.

Another form of certificate, related to accreditation based on workplace experience rather than on assessment in schools and colleges, is offered by the YTS profile. This illustrates the implementation of policies which, in recent years, have called for formal qualifications for all (not just the "academic"), for such qualifications to relate to the competences required in work, for encouragement to young people and adults to build on these qualifications and for employers to give them proper recognition.

The ubiquitous modular form appears in this work-based accreditation, but the substance of the modules presents greater problems in contexts where there is no curriculum to which they can be "nailed". The competences encompassed by the modules must be concerned with what is of use in the workplace, but the aim is to concentrate for accreditation purposes on those which are generalisable or industry-specific rather than on those which might be described as company-specific. There is, unfortunately, a reluctance on the part of some industries to recognise qualifications below that of craftsman and this has not assisted the development of accredited ROAs and may, indeed, adversely affect the value placed on them by young people and employers.

Within the more traditional areas of certification there have been profound changes which have greatly increased the proportion of the population for whom certification is designed. At the end of compulsory schooling, Standard Grade is now available in the form of two year courses for all pupils in mainstream (and some special) education, with assessment relating to three broad bands of achievement and with certification at sixteen. The increase in the areas of the curriculum which are now the province of certification through Standard Grade has been designed to offer opportunities for the recognition of achievement well beyond the traditional, and more academic, scope of certificates in the past.

The National Certificate (which relates primarily to non-advanced further education but is making some in-roads in to secondary schools' curricula at earlier stages) has replaced a confusing and cumbersome conglomerate of courses and certificates with a modular curriculum and single accreditation system. Some of the modules are general in nature, but others are of a specialist kind which provide the building blocks of vocational qualifications. Those young people who for various reasons attempt or are successful on only a small number of modules, still get credit and recognition for what they have achieved. The scheme is designed to be flexible in a way which allows it to be used by a large proportion of the population for many purposes relating to vocational training and personal development. The effectiveness of the implementation of the system, the quality of the moderation procedures, the real choices and chances it provides for the individual and the readines of industry and commerce to use it efficiently and wisely, will all be major influences on whether this new opportunity for widespread certification achieves its undoubted potential.

In Conclusion

The diverse contributions to this book have attempted to give the reader a flavour of the various dimensions of the changes which have overtaken assessment in the education and training of young people over the last ten years or so. Perhaps the most fundamental change has been the recognition that assessment, for whatever purpose, must be about providing the best possible accounts of what the individual (or sometimes the group) knows, can do or has experienced. No longer is the main emphasis on making a precise *measurement* of something which will result in a simple judgemental mark or grade.

In some circumstances the "best possible account" may still include some measurement, but it could equally well take the form of a narrative report of the knowledge and skills acquired by a young person. In an ideal world, the form the account takes should be tailored specifically to that young person; in the real world, that is not always possible because of the large numbers of individuals who have to be assessed. The problems of managing individual-ised reports across the country for certification, or even across a class of any size, would be profound. Nevertheless, it is increasingly recognised that any common framework for assessment must be sufficiently flexible so that relatively detailed information about the individual can be included, and in the case of assessment for real diagnostic purposes there is no escape from the requirement of complete individualisation.

The increasing use of more descriptive assessment has had considerable implications for the reporting of achievements. To report at the end of a course on every achievement for each young person would produce an unmanageable document which users (e.g. parents, employers, other educational institutions) would probably reject. The design and production of forms of report which are sufficiently succinct to be valued and used by readers, and yet provide enough additional detail and meaning to be seen as desirable replacements for marks or grades, is one of the major challenges to the assessment innovators. But effort also has to be made on the part of the users; no longer can one simply count up grades or marks; now it is necessary to look at the *meaning* of what the report says about the achievements and ask whether those achieve-ments match what is required and taken-for-granted of the young person for the job, career or course to which he or she aspires. Administratively speaking, making use of assessment is now much more complex than in the past; where it used to be a simple *procedure* (e.g. "2 Bs and a C will get you into course X") now it is seen as a *process* requiring several stages and substantial intellectual input.

Our ideas about the process of assessment itself, however, have undergone even more major reforms. For many people the trio of processes, teaching–assessment–learning, are now integrated into a system in which the traditional distinctions of the one who teaches, the one who learns, the one who assesses, the one who asks the questions, the one who answers the questions and so on are no longer so clear-cut. The notions of young people's self-assessment, the importance of teachers learning about the schemata which children develop in their long-term memories, and the integration of assessment into teaching rather than being manifest as end-of-unit testing, are each indicators of this trend. Assessment is no longer seen as an end in itself; it has to earn its keep by contributing to the effectiveness of the education and training which is offered to young people. And it is that criterion on which it should be judged.

THE AUTHORS

SALLY BROWN (editor) is the Director of the Scottish Council for Research in Education. A former physics teacher and lecturer, she has been in educational research since 1970. Most of this time was spent in a university department of education, but for a period of four years she was seconded to the Scottish Education Department with responsibility for a major research programme, much of it associated with assessment. Her current interest is in research into teaching; previously her research and publications have been concerned with science education, teachers' and pupils' attitudes, factors influencing the effectiveness of curricular innovations, pupils' cognitive preferences, criterion-referenced assessment and educational research policy.

HARRY BLACK is a senior research officer at the Scottish Council for Research in Education where he has worked since 1977 on a programme of assessment projects. His particular interest is in applications of criterion-referenced assessment and especially its use for diagnostic purposes. He has written widely on the subject and his paper for this book is based largely on his current research into assessment in the Scottish National Certificate. Current and past research for which he has had major responsibility include the evaluation of a local authority assessment initiative, a study of an EEC-funded transition to adult life project, Scottish evaluations of TVEI, and a range of smaller-scale studies for local authorities.

JULIE BOWEN taught at Stevenson College of Further Education after carrying out research in Psychology at

Edinburgh University. Her work included assessment training for staff from Social Work and further education, and through her classes for mentally handicapped adults she developed an interest in the assessment of learning difficulties. In 1978 she moved to Fife to set up provision for students with special needs in the region's four further education colleges, and later became Project Leader for a national project on learning and assessment in the Youth Training Scheme. She has also co-ordinated 16+ Action Plan developments, run ESF sponsored courses for women and disabled people, had a responsibility for staff development as TRIST Coordinator and been Planning Coordinator for TVEI Extension in Fife. Currently she is one of the three TVEI advisers for Scotland. She is a co-author of *Assessment in Youth Training Made to Measure?*

ERIC DREVER is lecturer in education at the University of Stirling with responsibility for research. After graduating from Glasgow University he taught science in Glasgow schools from 1962 to 1972, and also worked as an examiner for the Scottish Examination Board. His main interests in research and teaching are in formal and informal criterion-referenced assessment; in the processes of teaching, learning and assessment in the mixed-ability classroom; in mastery learning and individualised learning; and in the processes by which teachers and student teachers develop their pedagogy.

LINDSAY MITCHELL is currently directing the Competency Testing Project at the Scottish Vocational Education Council (SCOTVEC). She graduated in sociology in 1975 from Exeter University and then worked in a variety of jobs including waitressing and clerical work before undertaking a PGCE in Primary Education. Since 1980 she has worked on a number of research and development projects, in several sectors of education, all with an assessment focus. The research has included the practical assessment of mathematics in the primary school, selection of aspirant teachers into colleges of education and the assessment of occupational competence. The last of these focused on the investigation of new contexts and forms of accreditation; in particular for the Youth Training Scheme, and in general to industry as a whole.

MARY SIMPSON is a psychologist whose early research interest lay in the study of the neural mechanisms of perceptions, recognition, memory and learning. She became involved in educational research at Northern College of Education (Aberdeen Campus) in 1976 when, with funding from the Scottish Education Department, she joined the biology staff in a series of investigations of the origins and diagnosis of the learning difficulties of certificate pupils in secondary science. She has subsequently completed two projects in assessment in Standard Grade subjects, but will be returning to the field of pupil learning with her next project, a study of differentiation in primary classrooms.